THE TOTAL FAMILY

The Total Family

EDWARD E. HINDSON

Tyndale House
Publishers, Inc.
Wheaton, Illinois

Pictured on the front cover
are Dr. Ed Hindson, his wife Donna,
and their children Linda,
Christy, and Jonathan.

LIBRARY OF CONGRESS
CATALOG CARD NUMBER 79-66818
ISBN 0-8423-7285-7,
PAPER
COPYRIGHT © 1980
BY ED HINDSON.
FIRST PRINTING, MAY 1980
PRINTED IN THE UNITED STATES
OF AMERICA

Contents

Preface

God has a plan for total family happiness and success. His plan is expressed in Psalm 103:17, 18: "But the mercy of the Lord is from everlasting to everlasting upon them that fear him, and his righteousness unto children's children; to such as keep his covenant, and to those that remember his commandments to do them." God has made a promise to you, your children, and your grandchildren. It is a promise which he intends to keep if you will keep its conditions. This book is an exposition of this promise along with practical explanations to make it work for you.

Books are written to express ideas and to meet needs. More books on the Christian family are being written today than ever before, because the need is so great. We are facing a virtual "war against the family." One million marriages end in divorce each year in America alone. We have the highest divorce rate in the history of the world. The threatening question is: "Will the family survive the twentieth century?"

The contemporary problems facing the family have challenged Christian writers to reaffirm the biblical teaching on marriage and family living. The wide selection of books on these subjects varies greatly. Many are very helpful and readable. However, some are too technical for the average reader; some are unnecessarily offensive to either male readers or female readers (or both); and some are based far too much on idealistic theory or the personal experiences of the author. Therefore, the present study is an attempt to briefly state the current issues facing the family and present biblical guidelines regarding these matters. The solutions recommended grow out of a ten-year family counseling ministry in which these principles have been personally presented to more than 5,000 people. In addition, this material has been taught to 500,000 individuals in local church family seminars across the United States and Canada during that same period.

The basic principles set forth in this study are as old as the Bible itself. They work simply because they are God's principles and he makes them work in the lives of those who will obey them. The human influence of Bill Gothard and Jay Adams on the author will be obvious to the reader. These two men have probably done more to further a truly biblical understanding of the family than anyone else in our lifetime.

Let me urge you to read these chapters with an open and discerning mind. If you are reading as a couple—whatever else you do—don't fight over what you have read. Read each section with a desire to improve your personal relationship to God and your family. Don't try to point out everyone else's mistakes. Remember, you cannot change others, but you can change yourself. As you begin reading, remember that you are the real key to success in your family. Whatever you do— right or wrong—will determine what everyone else in your family does. Do not look for new areas to nag others about. Concentrate on yourself. Look for areas of your own life that can be improved. Face your failures and determine to correct them. Learn to trust God's principles; they have worked for centuries.

Dr. Ed Hindson
Director of Counseling, Thomas Road Baptist Church
Professor of Religion, Liberty Baptist College
Lynchburg, Virginia

1/The Ultimate Plan:
The Total Family

A few weeks ago a well-dressed, middle-aged woman sat in my office and said, "I'm tired of having half a family . . . I want a total family! A *total family* is one in which every member fully participates in his relationship to every other member. Such a family has a dynamic leader for a father, a creative, self-sacrificing mother, and cooperative children who respect what their parents represent.

THE FRACTURED FAMILY

The American family is disintegrating. With one million new divorces every year, some sociologists are even wondering if the home is going to become obsolete! Television programs now glorify the broken family, the single parent, the "necessity" of divorce and its acceptance by well-educated, discerning people. Almost every aspect of the media implies that this is the new American life style. Interviewers would have us believe that life is more fun after a divorce—in spite of the fact that all psycho-sociological tests indicate the opposite!

There is only one ultimate reason why the family is failing today. God himself instituted the family. He has the only successful plan for family living. Whenever his plan is followed, the family benefits from his blessing. When his plan is rejected, the family fails. Humanistic attempts to restructure the family with "open" marriages, conditional contracts, group therapy, and reversed roles have all failed miserably!

Some, then, will ask why the "traditional" family has failed also. The more traditional family is patterned after the Christian model and it cannot work without Christ. The historic impact of Christianity upon early American culture has left secularized modern America with many vestiges of Christian custom and morality. For example, it is still very popular to conduct a wedding in a church, whether the bride and groom have any kind of commitment to Christ or not. In reality, though, a church wedding is not necessarily a real Christian wedding.

A GENUINE CHRISTIAN FAMILY

A truly Christian wedding is one which recognizes the genuine spiritual unity of two born-again believers. A wedding and the ensuing marriage are not uniquely "Christian" because the pastor is a Christian. A distinctively Christian marriage is such because both the husband and wife are born of God!

The Apostle Paul said to the Christian couple: "Submitting yourselves one to another in the fear of God" (Eph. 5:21). Both the husband and the wife must surrender the control of their lives fully to the Lord and to each other. Marriages fail because partners are not totally committed to one another. A lack of such total commitment causes many young married people to give more time and attention to their jobs, home, hobbies, activities, status, etc. Some couples spend more time and money on their wedding than they do on their marriage.

God's plan for a successful family must begin with a total surrender of two lives to one another and then to God himself. Anything less than this will lead to conflicts, arguments, and frequent tensions. Only a total giving of yourself to your mate can place you in a position to fulfill all your responsibilities within marriage. Too many people marry for wrong reasons and their "expectations" are destroyed by the reality of life.

TWO-HEADED FAMILIES

Somebody once said, "Anything with two heads belongs in the zoo!" That includes your family. Two-headed families are as confusing as they are clumsy. In the San Diego Zoo, there used to be a sign next to a two-headed snake which read: "Animals with two heads lack the intelligence to cooperate with themselves and will die at an early age." The same principle is true of the two-headed family. When no final authority structure exists in a family, confusion and arguing result. "But Dad, Mom said we could go," argue the kids. "But I said you couldn't," snaps Dad. A verbal battle follows to determine who will get his way. Family life can often be a struggle of wills. If allowed to run its own course, this struggle will destroy the family and alienate each member from the other.

God's plan for the family is quite different. The Bible clearly states that the wife is to submit to her husband's leadership and help him fulfill God's will for his life (cf. Eph. 5:22-24; Col. 3:18). There can be no doubt of what these passages mean. She is to submit to him just as she would submit to Christ as her Lord. This places the responsibility of leadership upon the husband where it belongs. In a sense, submission is learning to duck, so God can hit your husband! He will never realize his responsibility to the family as long as you take it. If you want your husband to be more of a leader, let go of the reins. Most men do not enjoy fighting their wives for control of the family, so they sit back and do nothing. In time, the wife may have a nervous breakdown trying to run something God did not call her to run.

THE HUSBAND IS THE KEY!

The same passages that command the wife to obey her husband, command the husband to love his wife! Being a leader is not being a dictator, but a loving motivator who, in turn, is appreciated and respected by his family. Dad, God wants you to be the loving heartbeat of your home by building the lives of your family through teaching and discipline. A total family does not just happen, it must be developed by following God's formula for the family. Effective male leadership is essential for family stability. The interrelationship of family members must center around the person of Christ, so that a total family is one that is in fellowship with itself. Inner unity strengthens the outward stability of the home. Do not settle for half a family; make it a total and dynamic fellowship of interpersonal relationships.

The Bible makes it clear that God has a plan for the successful family. The Creator of life certainly did not establish the family to be a failure. Families are failing because they are violating God's principles for family success. Those principles begin with the relationship of husband and wife. Only when they properly fulfill their roles within marriage can their marriage be a blessed success.

THE FAMILY . . . GOD'S PLAN OR YOURS?

According to the New Testament Scriptures, the father is chosen of God to be the head of the home. The firm and loving leadership of a father builds a canopy of protection over his wife and children. As the husband takes the pressure of various decisions, he protects his family by relieving them of that pressure. The wife who tries to lead the family (deliberately or of necessity) finds herself under a great emotional strain that God never intended her to bear.

Some men mistakenly interpret the Scripture to teach that they are to be dictators in the home. This is not so. God has called a man to be the leader and the head, not the dictator. Those who cannot lead usually dictate. A Christian wife and her children will gladly follow a man who is following the Lord. In 1 Timothy 5:8, the husband is depicted as the provider for the family. In Mark 3:27, he is portrayed as the protector. In Deuteronomy 6:6-12, he is the priest or the spiritual leader of the family.

PRIVILEGE BRINGS RESPONSIBILITY

With the privilege of leadership comes the responsibility of leadership. Since the beginning of time (with Adam), God has given the husband headship over the wife. This position does not need to be taken by force since it has already been God-given. Headship in the family is taken by simply assuming the responsibilities of leadership. "Likewise ye husbands, dwell with them according to knowledge, giving honour unto the wife, as unto the weaker vessel, and as being heirs together of the grace of life; that your prayers be not hindered" (1 Pet. 3:7). Here we find three basic functions clearly emphasized.

1. *Leadership in knowledge.* Every wife has a basic need to find security in her husband's knowledge of life, of her, of God. Often while listening to the evening news, the wife will ask, "Honey, what does that mean?" She probably already knows, but she wants to hear her husband say, "It is all right; I have the problem under control." She needs the security of her husband's leadership in this area.

"Knowledge" does not necessarily mean intellect or education. The husband's leadership should reflect wisdom and discernment. Spiritually, he must lead the family in knowing God through his Word. His ever-growing knowledge of the Lord will draw his family closer together. It needs the security of his leadership in family devotions.

2. *Leadership in honor.* The husband should respect his

God-given position of authority by treating those under him with respect. This means he must speak honorably to and of his wife. There is no room for sloppy or dirty language when referring to the spiritual partner God has given him for life.

3. *Leadership in sharing.* "Being heirs together of the grace of life" indicates the responsibility of the husband in the matter of spiritual growth. He is responsible to God not only for himself, but for his wife and children. Sharing with each other will build spiritual stability in the home. Again, the husband is to take the leadership in meeting this need. If he is failing his family, then his prayer life is failing also ("lest your prayers be hindered"). No man can progress in the quality of his service to God through the church without first making progress at home. In fact, failure at home can disqualify him from serving in the church (cf. 1 Tim. 3).

SUBMISSION AND SUCCESS

"Wives, submit yourselves unto your own husbands as unto the Lord" (Eph. 5:22). The Bible's direction for the wife is as clear as any statement in Scripture. She is to submit to her husband's leadership in the same way and to the same degree that she would submit to Christ as Lord of her life.

Over the centuries, nothing has done more to elevate the status of women in society than the impact of Christianity. In those countries where the gospel has made little penetration the woman still has a very subservient position. This is not so in the areas where Christianity has taken root. The Bible makes it clear that a women can be just as saved and just as spiritual as a man. She is a sister in Christ, to be treated with dignity and respect.

In the home however, the Bible also makes it clear that there should be one "head," or final authority. The Christian wife is to recognize this "headship" in her own husband. When there is no final source of authority in the family, all differences of opinion must be settled by arguing. This teaches the children to argue as well, instead of obeying their parents. The wife is the most important family member in setting an atmosphere of either tension or cooperation.

As a woman, it will be necessary for you to come to the spiritual maturity of learning God's principle of submission. Learn to accept your position in the home as an opportunity for personal fulfillment and creative involvement with your husband and children. A family at war with itself can never become a total family. Such a family will produce a frustrated husband, a nervous wife, and insecure children who are suffering the consequences of their parents' conflicts.

THE TOTAL FAMILY PLAN

In order to be successful as a family it is necessary to understand and accept the basis of the family's authority. The family unit is not just a biological and social necessity. The Bible makes it clear that God himself instituted the family in giving Adam and Eve to one another in marriage (Gen. 2:18-25). When God brought Eve to Adam, it was "love at first sight." Adam immediately accepted her. He did not ask God if he could not have done better. She was the ideal wife, perfectly suited (that is the literal meaning of "help meet," v. 18) to his needs. He was the ideal husband, perfectly designed to meet her needs.

In response to this first marriage, Scripture states, "Therefore shall a man leave his father and his mother, and shall cleave unto his wife: and they shall be one flesh" (v. 24). That is to say, they shall be *total*. This "total couple" was to be spiritually, emotionally, and physically united to one another. Theirs was to be a relationship of total unity. In marriage, the husband is to make a clear break with his family ("leave") and is to establish a totally new family relationship

("cleave") with his wife. She, not his mother, must now become the number one woman in his life.

LEVELS OF AUTHORITY

The same God who instituted marriage and the family has also given us clear directions as to how the family is to function. In spite of the deep personal unity between Adam and Eve, the man was still clearly designated by God as the "head" of that family. The husband was the immediate authority, while God himself was the ultimate authority. Therefore, sin did not enter the human race when Eve sinned, but when Adam sinned. Notice that Romans 5:12, 14 clearly states: "By one man sin entered into the world, and death by sin; and so death passed upon all men . . . after the similitude of Adam's transgression." The Apostle Paul refers to Adam's being created first as the basis of male leadership (1 Tim. 2:12-14).

GOD'S CHAIN OF COMMAND

God has established three basic institutions on earth and has promised to honor each one. They are vitally interdependent and when one fails, they all suffer. These institutions are:

Human Government (Rom. 13:1-5)

Local Church (Heb. 13:7, 17)

Total Family (Eph. 5:22-6:3)

The Bible makes it clear that each of these institutions derives its authority from God himself, as he reveals his will through his Word. Therefore, God himself is the highest authority in his "chain of command" and all earthly rulers derive their authority from him (see diagram). God himself is the ultimate standard for our lives, and his standards are revealed his Word. All civil, religious, family, and personal leadership must acknowledge and submit to God's authority in order to function properly. Since God has revealed himself and his truth through Scripture rather than direct signs, we must recognize that obedience to his Word brings submission to his authority. One should never try to evaluate God's will for his life by circumstances and conditions (for example, "if it does not rain today, I will know that God wants me to get married"). One does not determine the will of God by feelings and circumstantial "signs." Rather, we can know the will of God by obeying God's Word.

God's Chain of Command

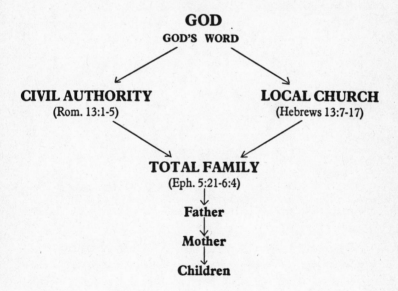

CIVIL AUTHORITY

The Bible clearly teaches the separation of church and state. That means that the church is to have authority over the spiritual affairs of our lives while the government is to rule over civil affairs. Throughout history, attempts to mix church and state authority have tended to lead to disaster.

Romans 13:1-6 makes it clear that the powers that be are "ordained of God" and are to be respected and obeyed by the Christian. The individual believer is to recognize the validity of governmental authority. He does not have the right to break the law, no matter how just his cause may seem. The importance of this concept is its effect upon the family's attitudes. Parents who continually criticize the government and look for ways to cheat it or misuse it are teaching their children to disrespect it also. The recent antiestablishment "revolution" was a good example of what this type of behavior can lead to. Remember, an example of contempt for authority will breed contempt for *your* authority in your children.

SPIRITUAL AUTHORITY

While recognizing the properly constituted authority of government, some have neglected to emphasize the authority of the pastor and the local church. Again, as in each level of the "chain of command," the parents' example will determine their children's attitudes. The Christian church member is to recognize the authority ("rule," cf. Heb. 13:7) that the church has over his life.

Hebrews 13:7, admonishes us to "remember them which have the rule over you, who have spoken unto you the Word of God . . . " The idea is to remember one's pastor, etc., with an attitude of respect for his position of authority. That means do not go home on Sunday afternoon and have "roast preacher" for dinner! Hebrews 13:17 emphasizes: "obey them that have the rule over you and submit yourselves: for they watch for your souls ..." Obedience to God-given authority over our lives develops the strength of character necessary to mature us into faithful servants of the Lord.

Most parents who complain that their children have lost interest in church admit that they have openly criticized their pastor and their church in front of their children. Again, they have reaped the negative attitudes they have sown in their children.

PARENTAL AUTHORITY

The effectiveness of the parents' authority over their children will be determined by the adults' attitude toward authority over them. Parents who contradict and criticize civil and spiritual authority are ultimately undermining their own authority. Children must learn to respect the ability of their parents to follow others, so that they may have confidence in their parents' leadership. Since the mother is in the middle of the family, she is the key to the children. Her submission to her husband's leadership teaches the child respect for his father and builds his sense of security within the family.

In Ephesians 5:21-24, the Apostle Paul, speaking under the inspiration of the Holy Spirit, tells us that a successful marriage begins with mutual submission of the husband and wife to one another under the authority of God. However, that is only the first of several essential steps toward a Christ-centered home. The Scripture goes on to say, "Wives, submit yourselves unto your own husbands, as unto the Lord. For the husband is the head of the wife, even as Christ is the head of the church: and he is the saviour of the body. Therefore as the church is subject unto Christ, so let the wives be to their own husbands in everything."

YOU CAN BE A "SUPER PARENT"

In the same passage the Word of God tells the husband just how to give the leadership his family needs (Eph. 5:25-28). You do not need a baseball bat nor a bull whip in order to be the leader in your home. Men who resort to yelling, screaming, or beating their wives are only admitting their failure as leaders. Indignant frustration is no substitute for wisdom and kindness. "Husbands LOVE your wives even as Christ loved the church and gave himself for it" (Eph. 5:25). The more you love your family and the more secure they are in your love, the more willingly they will follow your leadership. In either case, Christ is the standard for the home: the wife submits to her husband as she would to Christ; the husband loves his wife as Christ loved the church.

SOMETHING TO THINK ABOUT

Whose plan for the family works best?

____ *God's plan*   ____ *man's plan*

Whose plan have I been following?

____ *God's plan*   ____ *man's plan*   ____ *some of both*

How well do you react to authorities outside the family (pastor, employer, policemen)?

____ *very respectful*   ____ *fairly cooperative*

____ *cooperate but complain*   ____ *very resistant*

How do your children react toward you?

How often do you criticize your church?

____ *some daily complaints*   ____ *weekly outbursts*

____ *occasional criticism*   ____ *no open criticism*

How often do your children criticize your church?

Have they started to object to attending services? ____

When you disagree with your children, do you:

____ *blow up*   ____ *claim own "right" to your opinion*

____ *direct their attention to a supporting principle in Scripture*

Now when your children disagree with you, what do they do?

Husband, rate your wife's submissiveness to your leadership.

_____ *openly and privately submissive* _____ *only submits part of the time*

_____ *only submits in public* _____ *very rebellious* _____ *rarely submissive*

Now, how do your children submit to both of you?

What immediate improvements could be made in implementing God's "chain of command" in your family?

2/The War Against the Family

THE RISING DIVORCE RATE

One million couples will divorce during the coming year! Sociologists now estimate that by the twenty-first century, the divorce rate in America will climb to 50 percent. Contrast this with the fact that the marriage rate is declining! The contemporary American family faces its most crucial days in the decade ahead. The "war against the family" has already begun!

The basic family unit has never been under such an attack in any society as it is today. Our popular television programs are continually promoting anti-family concepts: abortion, divorce and remarriage, adultery, sex without love, premarital sex, rebellion against authority, etc. The "war against the family" has already begun! The Apostle Paul predicted: "In the last days perilous times shall come; for men shall be . . . disobedient to parents . . . (2 Tim. 3:1, 2). Never since the days of Noah has there been a "war" on the family as there is today. Newsmedia, literature, television, movies, education, and even religious organizations are attacking the family. Several critics of society now believe that the family may not survive the twentieth century (cf. A. Tofler, *The Fractured Family*).

CULT OF THE PLAYBOY

Wars involve weapons and Satan's contemporary arsenal is awesome. The "playboy philosophy" has swept America.

Playboy is the best-selling magazine nationwide. It is only one of dozens of magazines of its type, presenting more than dirty pictures . . . it promotes a lifestyle that says, "down with the family!" One will never find an article in these magazines on how to be a better husband or how to develop a successful family. Trends such as "open marriage," promiscuous sex, wife-swapping, etc., are increasing evidences of the power of this "cult."

WOMEN'S LIBERATION MOVEMENT

The "feminist revolution" is nothing more than a female counterreaction to the "playboy philosophy." The very women who scream that they are being mistreated by male "chauvinist pigs" dress immodestly and live immorally. It is no wonder they are being mistreated! Check the magazines of this movement *(Playgirl, Cosmopolitan, Vogue)* and again you will find nothing supporting the family, motherhood, submission, or decency. The afternoon TV "soap operas" continue to spin their themes around sexual frustration, adultery, divorce, remarriage, and failure. Again, no help is given to the woman seeking to be a godly wife and mother.

HOMOSEXUAL REVOLUTION

The so-called "gay" liberation has become another weapon in Satan's arsenal of attack against the family. The homosexual revolution has become an increasingly vocal movement. With the failure of male leadership, we would expect an increased number of male homosexuals. They are normally the product of a dominant mother and a weak, recessive father. Society continues to play down the seriousness of this problem. Unisexual clothing and hairstyles continue to break down the God-given distinction between male and female. The emphasis ultimately is the same: "Down with the family!"

QUESTIONABLE MEDICAL "ADVANCES"

Though science and medicine have made substantial contributions to society, they continue to say, "Don't ask any moral questions." The legalization of abortion now means that more babies are aborted every year than are born! Artificial insemination of babies is becoming common. Two hundred and fifty thousand such children are now living in the United States. In a recent article in *People* magazine, an appeal was made to continue legalizing AIDs (artificial insemination donors). By this means, a wife may conceive a child from another man's semen without any legal restriction! The end result will be the total fragmentation of "impersonal" families in which the children are artificially produced from other people's reproductive elements. They will have no real parents and thus will become the property of the state.

Christians often sit back thinking, "This can't happen." But it is already happening. In 1974, there were 970,000 new divorces in the United States alone. In 1975, we topped the one million mark for the first time in the history of the world! Every year since then has seen the addition of more than one million new divorces. The "war against the family" is already underway.

THE FAMILY AND THE MORAL CRISIS

One million American teenagers will become pregnant this year and 600,000 will abort their babies. In many of our major cities abortions outnumber births. Promiscuous sex is advertised on almost every street corner of our major urban centers. Lewd pornography tantalizes with "ultimate" sex thrills, topless girls, live sex acts, erotic homosexual activity, etc. The morality crisis has reached its peak in America. We cannot wait any longer to speak out against the avalanche of corruption that is threatening the moral and emotional stability of our nation.

History is filled with examples of nations and empires that fell as a result of moral decay and inward corruption. The Bible reminds, "Blessed is the nation whose God is the Lord" (Psa. 33:12). The ancient Hebrew prophet Isaiah warned Israel over one hundred years in advance that she was about to fall because of a decline of spiritual leadership. He predicted:

> *"For, behold, the Lord, the Lord of hosts, doth take away from Jerusalem and Judah . . . the mighty man, and the man of war, the judge, and the prophet, and the prudent, and the ancient, the captain of fifty, and the honorable man, and the counsellor, and the cunning artificer, and the eloquent orator. And I will give children to be their princes, and babes shall rule over them . . . as for my people, children are their oppressors, and women rule over them" (Is.3:1-4, 12).*

The great prophet went on to predict his nation's complete destruction by her enemies, because he knew that she did not have enough strong male leadership to reverse her downward moral slide. While these words were historically intended for the people of ancient Judah, they have a striking parallel to our own day. We too have a lack of strong spiritual leadership today in our military, judicial, social, and spiritual realms. It is no longer a matter of honor to serve in the armed forces. The average American distrusts political and judicial leaders. A credibility gap of respect exists between young people and the adult generation. Where are our honorable, wise old men today? We have none! We have to go back in history to George Washington, Abe Lincoln, or Teddy Roosevelt to try to revive the concept of authoritative American leadership. Decency and respect for one's fellowman are being swept away by the tide of moral corruption. Politicians, psychologists, preachers, and law agents are rationalizing their own indulgence in sin and defending the "right" of others to do the same.

DECLINING MALE LEADERSHIP
AND THE FALTERING FAMILY

The national divorce rate in the United States is now beyond the 40 percent mark. There are now more television programs about divorced families than married families. The newsmedia tend to imply that "mature adults" accept such things as "normal." Those who voice a different opinion are often maligned as "extremists" and "bigots."

America is in trouble today because the home is in trouble; and the home is faltering because men are failing to give their families responsible leadership. Men have led the headlong rush into hedonism and, therefore, are often too guilty to deal with moral problems in their own home. How can a father properly guide his children when they are fully aware of moral failure in his own life? Dad, you cannot watch lewd television programs, laugh at dirty jokes, yell at your wife, read pornographic magazines, and expect your children to respect your leadership.

Men are the key to a moral revolution in America. Men have led women and children the wrong way. Now it is time for an "army" of spiritually concerned men to lead us the right way! We need husbands who will love their wives and children with a total commitment of themselves. Dad, you do not really show your children that you love them when you compromise with sin. Nor can you possibly meet the needs of your own wife if your heart is filled with lust toward other women.

MORAL SUICIDE AND THE NEXT GENERATION

Children spend most of the early years of their lives imitating or reacting to their family environment. The first five years of a child's life are especially crucial in forming his learning patterns and his character development. Most children are the "victims" of their parents' weaknesses. Lack of discipline, "double standards," and moral laxity in the home will affect the lives of your children.

When parents "justify" sin and immorality, they commit a "moral suicide" that becomes the "genocide" of the next generation. The problem of physical child abuse has rightly received a great deal of public attention recently. But it is time that we exposed the problems of spiritual child abuse and parental neglect.

Children are the greatest natural resource of the United States. Our future lies in the hands of our children. Everything we hope to become must be accomplished through them. On my way to work the other day I saw a junior high school boy sitting on a pile of books, waiting for a school bus. He was intently practicing his trumpet. Though he was probably irritating the neighbors, I admired his ambition and desire for excellence. This boy made me feel good about our future.

I have heard about runaway children. They are attracted to cities like Washington, D.C., Atlanta, Dallas, and Los Angeles. Many of these children arrive in a strange town friendless, penniless, and despondent. Men lurk around bus stations and street corners where these runaways gather. They offer these kids companionship and security—something they didn't get at home. Before they know it, these boys and girls are caught up in prostitution. They destroy their futures in a few reckless moments.

I am concerned about the way Americans ruin their children. Television and movies glamorize prostitution. It is becoming increasingly evident that soon many states will attempt to legalize sex for sale among consenting adults. I am against it because God calls it a heinous sin. We all ought to oppose prostitution because it destroys young people.

But this is only one of many problems. Our children are ruined in other ways. I am concerned that between 200,000 and 300,000 Americans become alcoholics every year. There are an estimated 450,000 alcoholics between the ages of ten and twelve. I am concerned that almost 40 percent of our nation's armed forces have some form of drug consumption. I am concerned about the suicides among young people each year.

Our young people are turning to drugs and alcohol, resorting to suicide in an attempt to escape problems they cannot face.

Society shoulders some of the blame. Materialism produces tensions and false values. Schools share the blame when they do not prepare children for life; they water down content and refuse to enforce rules of human decency. The media, including movies, television, radio, and the publishing trade are guilty of promoting sensationalism, violence, sex, and permissiveness without accountability.

I believe the major problem stems back to the home, or the lack of one. Since the child is the extension of the family, the problem with our youth goes back to the fountainhead. We should place the blame there.

One of the most neglected and disobeyed verses of Scripture is Proverbs 22:6, "Train up a child in the way he should go: and when he is old, he will not depart from it."

We live in a permissive society which teaches that wrong is not always wrong and right is not always right; a society where truth is not eternal and we can "fib" to get ahead. This same society suggests that the family does not necessarily have to be the closely knit structural unit that it was just a few generations ago. In some counties, there is an appointed public official to defend the rights of children. Are we moving into a society where fathers and mothers no longer have the ultimate responsibility for their children?

Our youth are shown by society that it is not necessary for them to work hard to earn a living. They can join welfare programs, get food stamps, and live off the government.

As a pastor with three growing children whom I love, I am concerned about proper training. I don't want to ruin my children. They are a heritage from the Lord (Psa. 127:3).

PARENTAL NEGLECT

If there is anything which hurts the relationship between a parent and a child and ultimately ruins the youth, it is neglect. Neglect of a child begins very subtly, passing almost unnoticed. The father of a family I know was so proud of his infant son. When he came home from work he went directly to the crib to kiss and love his son. As the baby grew older, however, he was not as "cute" to his father and mother; they gave him less and less attention. He was often left alone. His parents allowed him to do whatever he pleased. In his teen years, he brought friends to the house during the day while both his parents were working. They drank the parents' liquor. Soon he brought girls to the house. One became pregnant. The friends got together and helped pay for an abortion. A year later, another girl friend got pregnant. This time, he could not persuade her to have an abortion; she had her illegitimate baby. From experimenting with sex he has gone to experimenting with drugs. He is now pushing dope on the streets of a major city and has long since departed from the church and from God. The father finally asked, "What did I do wrong?" But it was too late; his child was already gone.

There are some parents who do not touch their babies at

all. Psychologists have learned that if a human baby is not hugged and cuddled, he will suffer psychological damage. Some scientists claim that in extreme cases, the child will even die.

One way you love a child is by praying with him and reading God's Word. If you refuse to have a regular time of family devotions in your household, you may be damaging your children more than you are aware.

Billy Sunday, the great evangelist from the first half of this century, is said to have wept in his old age because he had won the masses, but lost his own children. They did not follow the old-fashioned religion he preached.

Some have paraphrased Mark 8:36, "For what shall it profit a man, if he shall gain the whole world, and lose his own children?"

That is why it is so important for me to spend time with my children. Granted, as a preacher of the gospel, I am extremely busy. But I try not to fool myself; I should never be too busy to spend time with my family and with each child individually. My wife's phone calls are always put through to me, regardless of what I am doing. At times, in order to make time for my children, I pull them out of school and spend time with them.

LACK OF DISCIPLINE

Recently I visited a Baptist seminary and met a student who proudly proclaimed, "I don't believe in corporal punishment." When he said that, I was disturbed, for that means he doesn't believe the Bible which teaches corporal punishment.

Notice what God has to say about discipline. "Chasten thy son while there is still hope, and let not thy soul spare for his crying" (Prov. 19:18). "He that spareth his rod hateth his son: but he that loveth him chasteneth him betimes" (Prov. 13:24). "Withhold not correction from the child: for if thou beatest him with the rod, he shall not die" (Prov. 23:13). "The rod and reproof give wisdom: but a child left to himself bringeth his mother to shame" (Prov. 29:15).

I do not believe in beating a child in anger to harm him physically. In love, the parent disciplines the child to teach him the correct lessons of life. One of the most tragic illustrations of lack of discipline in the Bible is that of Eli, priest at Shiloh, whose household was cursed "because his sons made themselves vile, and he restrained them not" (1 Sam. 3:13).

Discipline is taught in the New Testament as well as the Old Testament. "For whom the Lord loveth he chasteneth, and scourgeth every son whom he receiveth" (Heb. 12:6). "And, ye fathers, provoke not your children to wrath: but bring them up in the nurture [or discipline] and admonition of the Lord" (Eph. 6:4).

If you refuse to correct your child it is a sign that you hate him, not that you love him. And he will grow up with a distorted view of right and wrong.

MORAL PERMISSIVENESS

Our children are constantly encouraged through movies, television, radio, and literature to do what is right in their own eyes. Through an onslaught of pornographic material, our children are exposed to a lustful presentation of the human body, free sex, homosexuality as an accepted life style, crime that pays, violence, drunkenness, and rebellion against our nation.

They are taught that there is no God and no hereafter; so they had better make the most of their lives down here.

We need to teach our children what the Bible says about morality. For example, homosexuality is now being presented as an alternate life style. Though they claim to be another poorly treated minority, homosexuals should not be equated with racial minorities. Homosexuals are regular practitioners of perversion; they are sinners in need of a Savior. We must love them and show them that Jesus Christ has the power to forgive and cleanse them of their terrible sin; but we must not accept their sexually twisted lives as normal. They are abnormal. Their greatest sin is not what they do to themselves, but what they do to others. Homosexuals prey upon the young. Studies have shown that a person is not born with preference to the same sex; he is introduced to the homosexual experience and cultivates a homosexual urge. Innocent children and youth are often victimized and become addicts to sexual perversion.

Pornography is mailed throughout the United States just as easily as postcards these days. Even little children are receiving "plain brown wrappers" in the mail, and if their parents do not inspect these mysterious packages, they may indeed be sorry one day.

There are some adult movie theaters which show graphic sex scenes twenty four hours a day. They appear to be as easy to enter as a dime store, if a person can just act eighteen years old. And if that isn't enough, the Hollywood industry repeatedly puts out "PG" and "R" rated films. The kids see these. Even some "G" rated films dabble with the occult and satanic matters.

Television is getting nearly as bad. Regular programs discuss and expose illicit sex, rape, drug use, and abortion. In some areas, cable companies are showing first-run movies without any editing—graphic sex and violence right on your TV screen.

Issues in our nation today continually question God's universal laws. Women demand equal rights and loathe being pushed into the biblical role of wife and mother. Women lobby for abortion on demand—making it all the easier for them to go to bed with someone who is not their spouse.

Consider these factors. You have a choice in the matter. You may either let worldly men teach your child their vile ways, or you may train up your child in the way he should go. But remember this: If you choose the second alternative, you have God's promise that when your child is old, he will not depart from the way.

FAILING TRADITIONAL VALUES

Perhaps more than any nation in history, the United States has a Christian heritage. How could the very nation that was swept by the great revival movements of the past two centuries become so corrupt and spiritually destitute in so little time? Old traditional American values, which retain earlier Christian convictions, are now being swept aside by moral neutralism and situation ethics. "Do your own thing," and, "If it feels good, do it," have become our modern moral slogans.

A man's actions are the result of his beliefs. As the twentieth century dawned, the influence of Darwinian evolution and Freudian psychology brought a new intellectual climate to our schools and universities. Man was now viewed as a complex and "glorified" animal. He was the result of the selective processes of evolutionary physical development. His mind was seen as a complex system of moral guilt and suppression. Secular psychology demanded a totally neutral stance on moral questions. Freud viewed God as an emotional crutch and religion as the source of man's greatest frustrations and from which, therefore, man must be released. It has taken more than half a century for these ideas to filter down to the street level of our society. Thus, our present moral crisis is the result of a process begun long ago.

Christian moral values only work when they are empowered by Christ himself. Too many adult Americans are attempting to hold onto the vestiges of Christian moral concepts without a personal relationship to Christ. "You are going to do this because my parents always made me do it," they shout at their children. But when challenged about why they believe a certain principle to be true, they often have no answer. Their Christian grandparents may have believed and practiced those principles effectively and translated them into rules for family living. However, the next generation may have only adopted the rules without personal commitment to the principles on which the rules were based. By the third generation the rules seem meaningless and are rejected.

This shift of moral attitudes may be readily observed in today's movies and television programs. In the old westerns, the "good guy" always lived a clean life, wore a white hat, and maintained a virtuous relationship with the heroine. He went out of his way not to kill people, because he respected life. In today's western movies, it is difficult to tell the "good guys" from the "bad guys." The hero now wears a black hat and usually needs a shave. He smokes thin cigars, sleeps with several different women, and kills twenty to thirty people per hour. He is only "good" in the sense that he is less bad than the other guys! This is actually an accurate picture of modern society. All moral issues are being neutralized by situational reinterpretation.

CHRISTIAN MORALITY AND
CHRISTIAN CONVICTIONS

There can be no real revival in America without a revival of true Christian morality. Today's churches are lowering their standards in a foolish attempt to accommodate the world and its philosophy. This has weakened their stand on vital moral issues. When the church has nothing to say to the world, it has lost its unique purpose for existing. We are to be a committed people with a mission to the world. When we attempt to be just like the world in our life style, we no longer have a mission.

There can also be no genuine revival of Christian morality without a clear-cut adherence to the convictions on which those morals rest. Too many so-called Christian songs and books reflect very little evidence of real Christian convictions. Contemporary evangelicalism has lapsed into a religion of accommodation, compromise, and convenience. Today's therapeutic Christianity advertises: "Trust Jesus; you'll feel better."

A NEW CRUSADE FOR RIGHTEOUSNESS

Feeling-oriented Christianity often lacks the moral fiber of spiritual conviction which is necessary to stand up against immorality and crusade for righteousness. We need a new crusade for righteousness today—crusade led by Bible-believing, Christ-honoring, right-living adults and young people who are more concerned about their spiritual convictions than their personal convenience. Throughout church history, Christians have made a major impact on their generation for the cause of righteousness and decency.

THE APOSTLE PAUL preached vigorously against the immorality of the first century Roman world.

MARTIN LUTHER brought about the Protestant Reformation by opposing the superstitions of the medieval world.

JOHN CALVIN established a democratic society to give man a free option to the oppression of the feudal system.

JOHN WESLEY preached a revival of holy living in response to the urban corruption of the Industrial Revolution in England.

JONATHAN EDWARDS stood against the idea of salvation by church membership and proclaimed the gospel of personal conversion which led to the Great Awakening in colonial America.

THE REVIVALISTS, like Asbury, Finney, and Moody, preached against the evils of slavery and immorality. They rallied

*their generation to proclaim Christian standards and convictions
throughout the nineteenth century.*

*BILLY SUNDAY came out swinging against the evils of alcohol
and rallied the temperance movement to oppose booze, bars, and
brothels.*

Then something happened. Since the middle of the twentieth century fundamentalist Christianity has been fighting for its survival and we have turned our attention away from the great moral issues of our day. The open display of pornographic literature and the blatant immorality of television and the movies are deceiving young people and destroying marriages—and we have said almost nothing! It is time for today's Christian generation to stand up on these major moral issues and speak out against the sin that is eating away at the very foundation of our nation. The ideals of a free democracy cannot survive in an immoral society. Christian moral values only work when they are personally empowered by the living Christ.

The moral crisis of the latter part of this twentieth century demands our response. But what can I do? you may ask. While you cannot change the world by yourself, you can change your family. As a husband and father, you must give your family the consistent example of strong male leadership in your own home. The hope of America today is strong Christian families. Determine to make your family a fortress of spiritual and moral strength against the shifting tides of moral change. Let the changeless truths of Scripture guide your family as you follow God's formula for success in a total family.

PICKING UP THE PIECES
OF A FAILING MARRIAGE

"I know we are both saved, but we just don't love each other any more," says a young husband. "Everything seems to be falling apart," laments his wife. Many times over, this scene has been repeated in my office. The conclusion is usually the same: "I guess we will just have to get a divorce!"

God did not save you in order to make you miserable. If you are truly born again, the Holy Spirit lives within you (1 Cor. 12:13). In whom the Spirit lives, he produces his fruit, and the first fruit of the Spirit is love! It is a contradiction of terms for a Christian to say, "I just don't love him." Jesus went so far as to say, "Love your enemies"!

Anyone lacking love in marriage needs to determine whether he is genuinely born of God. God is the source of all love, and he gives that love to his children. You may have so sinned against the Holy Spirit that you have grieved him and restricted his fruit of love. If you are a genuine Christian, you can learn to love anyone . . . especially your God-given life partner!

DO NOT BE DECEIVED!

Many depressed couples become deceived into thinking that they may have married the "wrong person." This is a tragic misconception. You must learn to trust the God of the circumstances of your life. A powerful scriptural example of this is seen in the life of Jacob. His choice was Rachel, but God's choice was Leah. As adverse as the circumstances of his marriage were, Jacob still should have accepted God's choice. Let me prove this to you. While at first Jacob loved Rachel and hated Leah, he later changed his attitude. When he died, he was buried with Leah, not Rachel. It was Leah, the mother of Judah, who became the progenitor of the line of Christ. She was definitely God's choice for Jacob. Learn to trust God's choices for your life.

ADMIT YOUR FAILURES!

One of the most difficult things you ever have to do in life is to admit by name your own personal failures. It is always easy to point out the mistakes of your mate. It is an entirely different matter to sincerely and honestly acknowledge your own failures. Stop being so self-righteous and filled with self-pity. Remember it "takes two to tangle." If your marriage is failing, it is because *both* of you are failing. Both of you need to recognize the wrong you are doing and sincerely ask each other's forgiveness (cf. "Solving Family Conflict").

LET GOD TAKE OVER!

If you are experiencing trouble at home, then God is not in control of your marriage! Stop trying to pretend otherwise. Stop trying to place all the blame on your partner. Finding a solution to your conflicts begins by admitting your own mistakes. You must yield your own personal "rights" to Christ and let him be Lord over your home. Surrender your lives to his control and the Holy Spirit will again produce the fruit of love in your hearts.

LIVE BY HIS PRINCIPLES!

Rebuilding your marriage begins with an attitude of repentance as you face your failures. Next, you must be willing to live by God's directions as revealed in his Word. Stop reacting in selfishness and learn to apply his "chain of command"; learn to forgive one another fully and completely. Be willing to obey every command of Scripture, knowing that obedience leads to blessing. Those things that are impossible with man are possible with God (Luke 18:27). He has an answer for every problem you face. Learn to trust his answers;

you will see him pick up the pieces of your failing marriage and reunite your hearts in his love.

SOMETHING TO THINK ABOUT

What are the greatest influences on our family at this time?

1 _____

2 _____

3 _____

4 _____

5 _____

What are we doing to reinforce good influences?_____

_____

_____

What negative influences are we allowing to go unchecked? _____

_____

_____

How could we change our course of action to better protect and encourage our children? _____

_____

_____

What moral habits and practices have changed in our family in the past five years? _____

_____

_____

Have these helped or hindered our family's spiritual growth? _____

_____

_____

_____

3/My Husband: The "Velvet-covered Brick"

"Daddy's home—he can fix it!" Johnny exclaims. "Wait till your father gets home—you are gonna get it then!" Mother warns. If you are like most fathers, you've put in a long, hard day before you walk through the front door and you may not be mentally prepared to be a fix-it man or a mean bear. The role of a father in our society has changed a lot since the beginning of this century. Once the aloof, autocratic provider, a father now finds he has a full-time job at home as well as at work. Your position in your home is vital to the stability and well-being of your wife and children. If you are fortunate, you have a job that you like, that pays well, and that gives you time with your family. Many men are not that fortunate and must learn to meet their family's needs in less than ideal situations.

"WHAT'S A FATHER FOR?"

The Bible reminds us: "Like as a father pitieth his children, so the Lord pitieth them that fear him" (Psa. 103:13). Throughout Scripture a father's responsibility to his family is continually emphasized. Of Abraham, God said, "For I know him, that he will command his children . . . after him" (Gen. 18:19). Jacob was commended for "blessing" his children (Heb. 11:21). Joshua declared, ". . . but as for me and my house, we will serve the Lord" (Josh. 24:15). God warned Eli that "[thou] honourest thy sons above me" (1 Sam. 2:29), and brought judgment on his family because Eli refused to deal with the iniquity he knew was there (3:13). There can be no doubt that God expects fathers to be spiritual leaders in their own homes.

During the wilderness journey, Moses became overwhelmed with the responsibilities of leading the nation of Israel and meeting the needs of each of its families. Therefore, God gave him a workable plan to expedite his leadership on every level. Moses was instructed to select a group of leaders (elders) whom he was to instruct. They, in turn, were to instruct the fathers, who then were to teach their own families. Thus, Moses was able to communicate his concepts, which were transferred down to every member of every family through the father's leadership.

WATCH OUT FOR THE ENEMIES OF SUCCESSFUL FATHERHOOD

Solomon observed: "A wise son maketh a glad father: but a foolish son is the heaviness of his mother" (Prov. 10:1). Fulfilling your parental responsibilities will bless you and failing them will curse you. Watch out for the "enemies" of your family.

1. *Occupation "Blues"*—Failure at work will tend to carry over into your family. If you are under pressure all day and are not handling it properly, you will often take out your frustrations on your family. This is why a Christian father must look upon his job as part of God's will and good purpose for his life. Working is not an end in itself. Nor should it become little more than a means of income. Our labor should be done unto the Lord, so that even our everyday tasks take on a spiritual significance. We are to accept our places in life and

do all things heartily as unto the Lord (Col. 3:23).

2. *Television "Blahs"*—Be careful of television; it will wreck you as a father. It is too tempting at the end of a rough day, when you are mentally exhausted, to just flop in front of the tube and turn off your brain. Too much TV will rob you of vital creative communication with your family. If you cannot control that "electronic monster"—unplug it! If you "flop" in front of the TV, you flop as a father!

3. *Devotional "Bores"*—Keep your family devotions fresh and alive. Get out of boring ruts. Stop reading the same passages over and over. Make sure that you are prepared— read the passage in advance. Learn to study the Scriptures for yourself and then teach them to your family. Become a real man of God to your family and give them the leadership they need. Remember, "He that troubleth his own house shall inherit the wind: and the fool shall be servant to the wise of heart" (Prov. 11:29). The very next verse declares: "The fruit of the righteous is a tree of life; and he that winneth souls is wise" (11:30). How is your "family tree" doing? Troubling your own house by failing to be a dad who leads will result in a whirlwind of conflict. By contrast, producing the "fruits of righteousness" in your life will enable you to win your own children to Christ. Your kids should want to become Christians because of the quality and character of your Chrisian life. They should not follow the Lord in spite of you, but because of you. To fail with your children is to fail at one of life's greatest opportunities.

YOU CAN BE A "SUPER DAD"

The Apostle Paul wrote: "And, ye fathers, provoke not your children to wrath: but bring them up in the nurture and admonition of the Lord" (Eph. 6:4).

A well-balanced father does more than just "bring home the bacon." He is a leader and teacher who motivates his children to effective decision-making. He is not afraid to correct them when they are wrong, nor does he demand behavior of them that he himself is not willing to give. The authoritative father loves his children enough to give them what they need, not just what they want. He enjoys listening to them and helping them with their special projects. He is in fellowship with God and shares that fellowship with his children. This kind of father may claim the promise of Scripture: "But the mercy of the Lord is from everlasting to everlasting upon them that fear him, and his righteousness unto children's children" (Psa. 103:17).

PRIVILEGE BRINGS RESPONSIBILITY

The husband's responsibilities are clearly defined in Scripture. He is to "leave" his father and mother and "cleave" unto his wife (Gen. 2:24). This is more than a physical description. He is to leave them emotionally as well. Your wife needs the security of knowing that she (not your mother) is the number one woman in your life. This, unfortunately, is often a real battle for young couples, as the wife struggles for equal recognition with a dominant mother-in-law.

The husband-father is also to be the priest-teacher of his family (Deut. 6:4-9). As God revealed his law to Moses he, in turn, taught it to the elders of Israel and they, in turn, taught it to the fathers, who were to teach it to their families. Even in the New Testament, the men were to carry the responsibility for spiritual leadership both in the church and in their own families (1 Tim. 2:8-15; 3:1-5; 1 Cor. 14:34, 35). This means that the husband must discipline himself to be a man of prayer and devotion (i.e., a man of God), so that he may lead his family out of the "overflow" of his own life. One cannot develop something in others which he has not built into his own life. Dad, you need to understand your wife and children and, by knowing their needs and limitations, design the kind of spiritual projects that will help them grow and develop spiritually to the glory of God.

Genuine marital unity is developed as a result of both the husband and wife accepting full responsibility for their complimentary functions in the family. The interaction of the husband's leadership and the wife's submission to his leadership brings the dynamic of unity and purpose to their marriage. However, the husband must always remember that good leaders are, first of all, good followers (for example, Joshua, Moses' servant, became the victorious leader of Israel). Jesus made it clear that for one to become a leader, he must be willing to be the servant of all (cf. Matt. 20:20-28). Our Lord himself became a servant that he might meet the needs of all men. In a similar way, the husband must be willing to become the servant-leader of his wife and children.

Leadership always brings responsibility. Too many husbands are running away from responsibility and yet are still trying to dictate to their families. A dictator is not a true leader. Real leadership sets the example and motivates others to follow that example. A leader must be a decision-maker, a teacher, and a motivator. He must be willing to delegate authority and responsibility within the family. He sets the ultimate moral and ethical guidelines for the family, but still allows each member the freedom to function within those guidelines.

The husband is actually commanded to love his wife (Eph. 5:25) as Christ loved the church with a volitional, unconditional, unselfish, and unending love. The Bible describes "love" as a spiritual quality, not just an emotional feeling. God places the responsibility for insuring love in the family's relationships upon the husband. Too many men complain that they feel unloved by their families. In reality, they feel that way because they have failed to love their families as

Christ loved the Church. Love that only takes and does not give is not really love at all! Learn to love by giving yourself wholeheartedly to your family. They need you and they need your love.

The Bible also tells us that the husband is to be the leader in promoting an atmosphere of sharing in the family. You need to love your wife by allowing her to share your life and your thoughts, your plans, goals, and ambitions. Some men never achieve the freedom to do this due to a conscience clouded by the guilt of sinful thoughts and desires. To be a real father, you must be willing to be a true spiritual leader. Only a real man of God can build a godly family.

SOMETHING FOR THE HUSBAND
TO THINK ABOUT

What responsibilities in the family do I most readily accept? _____

_____

_____

_____

What responsibilities do I tend to avoid?_____

_____

_____

How are these affecting the overall condition of our family?_____

_____

_____

Does my wife continually ask me questions that I am not really answering?_____

_____

_____

_____

Am I genuinely meeting her need for the security of my knowledge? _____

_____

_____

In what ways do I wish she would improve her communication with me?

____ *talking*   ____ *sharing*   ____ *spiritually*   ____ *sexually*

How must I first be willing to improve my communication with her?

____ *talking*   ____ *sharing*   ____ *spiritually*   ____ *sexually*

Do I really show love to her in the ways that are important to her?

List these ways:

_____

_____

_____

Now, have your wife check the list!

4/My Wife: The "Fulfilled Woman"

In God's plan for our families, it is necessary that there be husbands and wives. There are some basic reasons (other than physical) why God planned for the home to have a loving cooperation of male and female.

HARMONY AND SECURITY FOR YOU

In the family relationships, each has a significant contribution to make toward the other. It is God's plan for the husband, as the leader, to take the pressures and responsibilities of leadership. This protects the wife and children from unnecessary pressure.

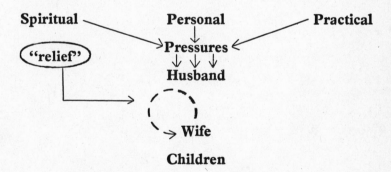

In the biblical plan for the home, the wife is actually in the "key" position. She has the opportunity of relieving many of her husband's pressures and thus further protecting the children. She does this through her housekeeping, shopping, praying, and sharing with her husband; and through the "ministry" of sexual relationship. If she is not submissive to her husband, she adds further pressure on him from within the home, causing him to overreact.

If the husband fails in the area of leadership, the pressure falls on the wife. When she "runs" the family she has no one between her and the children to relieve her pressure (so she takes it out on the children).

Pressures
↓ ↓ ↓
Husband⟵— — — **Wife**
↓
Takes out her frustration
on the children
↓
Children

Submission to your husband's leadership is not taking a second-rate position. It is a God-given opportunity to experience the genuine fulfillment of being a woman. God's plan for the home is one that brings harmony, unity, and the security of loving relationships. Take the challenge of your opportunities as a wife and your life will take on the depth of meaning and significance that God has planned for you. Be prepared for a blessing!

"WHAT IF YOUR HUSBAND ISN'T SAVED?"

"What can I do to reach my unsaved husband?" This question is often repeated by concerned Christian women everywhere. Usually they are looking for a "magic" answer to get their husband to Christ. Perhaps a better question would be, "What does God need to do in my life in order to reach my husband?"

Often the greatest change needs to be worked in the wife first, so that the husband may be attracted to the glory of Christ in her life. It has been my experience over the years that most wives who have unsaved husbands have violated some of the basic principles of Scripture. Often they end up "driving away" the man they once loved.

What goes wrong? Many times the newly saved wife exuberantly shares her discovery of Christ with her husband. He may not respond immediately and she may feel the urge to pressure him for an "instant decision" (forgetting that she did not make an instant decision herself). This puts an unnecessary barrier between wife and husband. The wife's Christianity may appear to be a "threat" to the husband's leadership. He may therefore resist her pleas to "be saved" simply because he does not want to be pressured into something he does not understand.

HELP HIM TO UNDERSTAND

Jesus made it clear in the "Parable of the Sower" (Matthew 13) that the true convert is one who hears the Word and understands it (v. 23). One must understand the basic elements of the gospel in order to be saved. As a wife, you can share these truths without "nagging" him into a response.

One of the greatest proofs of the truth of the gospel will be the change he sees in your life. "Therefore, if any man [or wife] be in Christ, he is a new creature: old things are passed away; behold, all things are become new" (2 Cor. 5:17). Can your husband see God's changing process in your life? Are your old habits and weaknesses passing away or does he still see you as the same old nagging, complaining, willful wife you were before you claimed to become a Christian?

WIN HIM WITH YOUR ATTITUDE

The Bible clearly tells the wife how to win her unsaved husband to Christ: "Likewise ye wives be in subjection to your own husbands; that if any [husband] obey not the word [of God] they also may without the word [from the wife] be won by the conversation of the wives" (1 Pet. 3:1).

Peter definitely tells the wife to obey her husband, even if he is disobedient to God's Word. This does not mean that she is to share in his disobedience, but that she is not to use her Christianity as an excuse to disobey him. Many naive Christian wives have driven their husbands away from Christ and the church because of a bitter and disrespectful attitude toward their unsaved husbands. You still have a God-given responsibility to love him and be the best wife possible to him. In 1 Pet. 3:4 we read that a "meek and quiet spirit" will win him to Christ, not a loud-mouthed obstinance. Proverbs 31 describes the "virtuous woman" as one who always speaks with wisdom and kindness (v. 26). Think of what it could mean to your family if every time you spoke it was with either kindness or wisdom. Let God win your unsaved husband by allowing him to change your life. When you become the godly wife the Lord intends for you to be, God will convict and change your husband through you—instead of in spite of you.

WHAT'S A MOTHER TO DO?

Proverbs 31

   10 *Who can find a virtuous woman? for her price is far above rubies.*
   26 *She openeth her mouth with wisdom; and in her tongue is the law of kindness.*
   27 *She looketh well to the ways of her household, and eateth not the bread of idleness.*
   28 *Her children arise up, and call her blessed; her husband also, and he praiseth her.*

30 Favour is deceitful, and beauty is vain: but a woman that feareth the Lord, she shall be praised.

"What's for dinner, Mom?" the kids ask. "Where's my sweater?" yells her husband. Mealtime is one of a mother's most hectic experiences each day. More things seem to go wrong at that one time than any other. As the pressures of your day mount up, you may often feel like you are going to crack. That's when you need to learn to pray. "Help, Lord; I'm a mother!"

Do some serious thinking for a moment. What does it mean to be a mother today? Women are finding their responsibilities far different than those of a mother of fifty years ago. You must now be an efficiency expert, economist, bargain hunter, affectionate lover, child guidance director, and communications expert. It is not easy to be a mother today in this rapidly changing world. Mothers are human beings whose contributions to the family are vital to its survival. Mothers deserve more credit than they usually receive for the sacrifices they make and for the inevitable problems they must endure for their family's sake.

THE IDEAL WIFE AND MOTHER

Notice in Proverbs 31:10-31 that the "virtuous woman" is intelligent, industrious, sincere, and submissive. She is described as being more valuable than rubies. She is so trustworthy that her husband is not seeking anyone else's attention. He enjoys being with her because she does him "good." She is creatively helping meet her family's financial needs as well as caring for the "poor" and "needy." She is well dressed so that her appearance enhances her husband's image of her. She is neither extravagant nor sloppy. She is feminine, yet competent. She can lead her children and follow her husband. She always speaks with wisdom or kindness and sets the atmosphere of blessing in her home. Thus her children call her "blessed," and her husband praises her because she honors God and her family.

MOTHERHOOD AND THE FAILING FAMILY

Now contrast the biblical picture of the ideal mother with the image of the contemporary woman with her alcohol, cigarettes, pills, nervous breakdowns, and generally disgruntled disposition. On television, "Maude" continues to shoot off her big mouth; the mother on "Family" dominates the scene; in "Soap" the mothers are either immoral or frigid; and in a host of programs bombarding the American home, motherhood in general is put down as an antiquated invention of the Victorians. No wonder our homes are in such desperate condition today.

RECAPTURING THE BIBLICAL ROLE

While the traditional role of the wife is being severely challenged today, we need to go back beyond mere tradition to the genuine biblical concept of motherhood. Her position in the home sets the example and pattern of respect for authority. Her attitude toward her husband will determine her children's attitude toward their father. A mother's place in the home is as significantly crucial as that of her husband, though he is the scripturally designated leader. The children will still develop their attitudes and life style from both parents.

CREATIVITY AND SUBMISSION

Children learn their essential concepts of security, independence, interdependence, and respect for authority from observing family members. Therefore, a wife's attitude toward her husband is vital to developing a healthy attitude in her children. They need to observe Mom's respect for Dad's position and leadership in the family. As she appreciates and accepts her husband's role in the family, the wife is preparing her children to do the same. Mom, your place in the family structure is extremely important to the well-being and stability of your family. Let God use you to be a blessing.

SOMETHING FOR WIVES TO THINK ABOUT

If your husband is not already saved, will your present attitude help bring him to Christ?

_____ *Yes* _____ *No*

What major things do you need to change now in order to reach him? _____

_____

_____

_____

How would you rate your husband's leadership?

_____ *excellent* _____ *very good* _____ *adequate* _____ *poor*

How would you rate your submission to his leadership?

_____ *excellent* _____ *very good* _____ *adequate* _____ *poor*

Now, is there a similarity between your submission and his leadership? Learn to be more submissive and he will become more of a leader!

What improvements could be made in your expression of submission to your husband? _____

_____

_____

_____

Now have your husband check the list!

5/The Total Parent: The Authoritative Balance

Recently two graduate students presented some interesting findings from their study of parent-teen relationships. They were attempting to discover why many young people do not follow the religious convictions of their parents. In the process of their study, they discovered that there are four basic types of parents. Their conclusions were interesting and revealing.

First, they asked several hundred teenagers to rate their parents in two specific categories: expression of love, and control. The ratings were to run from 0 to 100.

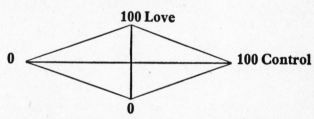

By recording their findings on a diagram like the one above, the graduate students soon realized that there were four basic types of parents:

NEGLECTFUL—low in love, low in discipline ... He avoids his children.

PERMISSIVE—high in love, low in discipline ... His children lead him.

AUTHORITARIAN—low in love, high in discipline . . . He pushes his children.

AUTHORITATIVE—high in love, high in discipline . . . He leads his children.

The balance of love and discipline proved to be the most important. The basic difference between the authoritarian parent (forced obedience) and the authoritative parent (motivated obedience) was one of approach toward discipline. As the students then interviewed and tested hundreds of young people from various backgrounds, the same patterns remained.

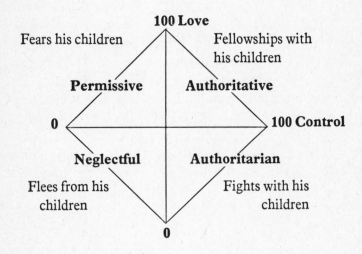

The results of their survey rated the response of young people to each type of parent, from strongest to weakest in each category.

I. Self-worth
1. Authoritative
2. Authoritarian
3. Neglectful
4. Permissive

Conclusion: Motivation to want to obey (rather than force) prompts obedience to others.

The Total Family

II. Response to "Authority"

1. Authoritative	Conclusion: Motivation to
2. Permissive	want to obey (rather than
3. Neglectful	force) prompts obedience to
4. Authoritarian	others.

III. Acceptance of Parents' Religion

1. Authoritative	Conclusion: Religious
2. Permissive	children reject ideals of
3. Neglectful	authoritarian parents.
4. Authoritarian	

IV. Acceptance of Parents' Life Style:

1. Authoritative	Conclusion: Teens reject
2. Permissive	life style of "pushy" parents.
3. Neglectful	
4. Authoritarian	

Notice that the children of "authoritative" parents had the highest rating in every category, whereas those of the authoritarian (discipline only) parents had the poorest rating in three categories. Remember that these findings do not negate the importance of discipline. Rather, they conclusively prove that discipline balanced with love is essential to effective parenting. Without that balance, discipline alone can be harmful. The biblical ideal is typified by God, our heavenly Father, who both loves and disciplines his children.

SOME CONCLUSIONS AND OBSERVATIONS

1. Discipline is essential, but without the balance of love, it is dangerous!

2. Love (without discipline) produces insecurity and poor self-image.

3. Both love and discipline are necessary in a proper balance to produce the best results.

Throughout the Bible, discipline is viewed as correction, not punishment (Prov. 22:15). Parental authority must always be tempered by loving concern for the child's ultimate well-being. Parents are never viewed in Scripture as mere biological necessities for the production of children. Parents are the responsible agents of God's authority in the family. They are to represent the character and love of God to their children.

HOW TO RAISE
EMOTIONALLY DISTURBED CHILDREN

The disintegration of the family unit is one of the major contributions to the rise of emotional disturbance among children. The bitter fighting and arguing of self-centered adults takes its toll on sensitive qualities of mental and emotional stability needed in family living. Dr. Paul Meier (*Christian Child-Rearing and Personality Development,* Baker) lists these qualities: love, discipline, consistency, parental example, and male leadership, as vital to an emotionally healthy family.

Children become the product of the home environment in which they are reared. A warm, secure atmosphere will produce a healthy self-image and personal confidence in a child. On the other hand, an atmosphere of tension and conflict will increase insecurity and heighten emotional conflict. Whether marital conflict leads to an actual divorce or not, it greatly reduces the probability of producing an emotionally healthy child.

TWENTY WAYS TO RUIN YOUR CHILDREN:

1. Spoil them by giving them everything they want.

2. Relieve them of all responsibilities by making all their decisions for them.

3. Nag and yell at them when they do wrong, but never spank them (it's out of date).

4. Foster an overdependence upon you so that drugs and/or alcohol can replace you when they are older.

5. Criticize each other openly so that your children will be totally confused over disciplinary matters.

6. Wife: dominate your husband so that your children will have no strong father image to respect.

7. Husband: blow up at everybody but refuse to help anyone with their problems.

8. Tell them how disappointed you are in their behavior, but do not correct it.

9. Do not assign any responsibilities through chores, etc. (you might overwork them).

10. Praise them for their looks or talent but not for their character.

11. Encourage your daughter to wear seductive clothing.

12. Reward your children whenever they play sick.

13. Do not keep your promises to them (they might believe you too much).

14. Never show any outward signs of love or affection, such as hugs and kisses.

15. Keep dirty magazines around the house (so your kids can grow up faster).

16. Overreact with extreme sympathy to every cut and scratch.

17. Talk all the time and never listen to them.

18. Be preoccupied with your own needs and neglect your children.

19. Never pray out loud with your children.

20. Get a divorce!

WHY DOESN'T THE CHURCH DO SOMETHING?

Unfortunately, most parents who violate God's basic rules believe that their children's problems are due to the failure of their church, pastor, youth group, or Christian school. Such shifting of blame reveals who these parents think is really responsible for rearing their children. It is utter foolishness for parents to think that they may push their children off on a day care center, a Christian school, or a youth group, and then continue to live contrary to what the group teaches. Proverbs 11:29 says, "He that troubleth his own house shall inherit the wind: and the fool shall be servant to the wise of heart." Proverbs 22:8 warns, "He that soweth iniquity shall reap vanity: and the rod of his anger shall fail."

God holds parents responsible for the spiritual development of their children (see Eph. 6:1-4). On the Day of Judgment, he will not accept any excuses about overbearing pastors or inept youth directors! He will evaluate the reality of parental love, example, and discipline.

APPLY GOD'S ANSWERS

The Bible is filled with advice about rearing children. Perhaps it is time you begin to heed it. You do not need to be afraid of what will happen to your children. Psalms 103:17,18 promises, "The mercy of the Lord is from everlasting to everlasting upon them that fear him, and his righteousness unto children's children; to such as keep his covenant, and to those that remember his commandments to do them." Here is a promise to your children and to your grandchildren. But you must be fully obedient in order to make the promise work. The more you obey God, the more your children will obey you.

The key to effective child discipline is always the parent, not the child. You must be willing to discipline yourself to teach and discipline your children consistently. "Discipline" is not just punishment, nor is it merely scolding; it is the complete application of corrective behavior in a disobedient child. Discipline never succeeds until it becomes correction.

TRAINING YOUR CHILD

Training involves instructing, but it includes more than that. When one trains a dog he does not merely talk to it. He usually applies the rolled-up newspaper! "Training" includes both instruction and discipline. In Ephesians 6:4, the Apostle Paul warns, "And ye fathers, provoke not your children to wrath; but bring them up in the nurture [discipline] and admonition [instruction] of the Lord."

When a parent does not balance his discipline with scriptural instruction, he will ultimately provoke his children to rebellion. A parent's discipline cannot be based upon personal opinion (the teenager will always challenge this). Instruction is the foundation of discipline and it must be based upon the Word of God.

DISCIPLINE IS NOT PUNISHMENT

The goal of discipline is correction. Any discipline that falls short of correcting the child's attitudes and actions is only a halfhearted attempt. Discipline cannot be given by mouth. When a parent finds himself trying to correct his children with hollering, he is failing. This is why the Bible clearly emphasizes: "spare the rod, spoil the child."

For the past two decades, psychologists have told parents not to spank their children. The result has been the most rebellious and irresponsible generation of young people who have ever lived in America. Now those same psychologists are saying that we ought to spank and discipline our children. Let the admonition of Scripture stand. "Foolishness is bound in the heart of a child: but the rod of correction shall drive it far from him" (Prov. 22:15).

YOU ARE THE ANSWER!

Attitudes and actions are learned, they are not "inborn." Your child's basic personality has been developed by his imitation of you. Often those things that displease parents most about their children are the very weaknesses of which those same parents are guilty themselves. We easily detect our own faults in others, especially our children. Do not be guilty of criticizing your youngster (or teenager) because he is turning out just like you!

Some parents constantly criticize their children with such statements as: "He is always bad, he cannot do anything right," or "Look at what a mess he is; what am I supposed to do?" You are actually admitting your own failure! Your child is what you have disciplined and trained (or failed to train) him to be. You are the "key" to his life. Trust God's promise and open the door of his blessing.

God has promised to bless your family and he will keep his promise to you. Proper discipline of your children begins by disciplining your own life. The Bible declares: "He that soweth iniquity shall reap vanity: and the rod of his anger shall fail" (Prov. 22:8). Do not be guilty of sowing sin in your own family. Sow righteousness and you will reap eternal blessings in the lives of your children.

HELP YOUR CHILD DEVELOP
A PROPER SELF-IMAGE

Self-image is what a person visualizes himself to be in regard to his appearance and abilities. When we talk about learning "self-acceptance," we do not mean that a person should be content with his weaknesses and failures. What we do mean is that he needs to learn to accept the unchangeable characteristics of his life (height, hair color, facial features, family background, etc.).

A poor self-image will affect one's attitude toward himself, family, friends, and God. A teenager with a self-acceptance problem, for example, will tend to shy away from friends or may move to the opposite extreme and become boisterous in order to gain attention.

There are two basic ways of developing one's self-image:

COMMAND

RIGHT WAY		*RESULTS*
Be conformed to IMAGE OF CHRIST	Understand and accept values God places on your appearance, abilities, parentage, and environment	RIGHT SELF-IMAGE: Confidence in God's design—self-acceptance

CHOICE

WRONG WAY		*RESULTS*
Be conformed to SOCIETY'S STANDARDS	Accepting values people place on your appearance, abilities, parentage, environment	WRONG SELF-IMAGE: Inferiority by comparison with others

SIGNS AND CONSEQUENCES OF WRONG SELF-IMAGE

1. Fears the will of God.
2. Resists authority (parents, church, etc.)
3. Hinders genuine friendships.
4. Uses wrong methods to gain "acceptance."
5. Overemphasis on materialism and fads.
6. Undue attention to physical appearance.
7. Difficulty in trusting God.
8. Wishing he was like someone else.
9. Lack of concentration (daydreaming).
10. Demands excessive attention by disobedience.

Solving the Self-Image Problem

Surface Problem (Visible)	Shyness Fear of People Withdraws from contact Self-criticism Depression
Surface Cause (Psychological)	INFERIORITY: From unfavorable comparison to others traits and abilities.
Root Problem	BITTERNESS: Toward God's design.
Root Cause (Sin)	PRIDE: Rejects God's purpose.

PSALM 139—GOD'S FORMULA FOR SELF-ACCEPTANCE

David, the psalmist, clearly expressed God's divine viewpoint regarding self-acceptance when he wrote:

"For thou has possessed my reins: Thou hast covered me in my mother's womb. I will praise thee, for I am fearfully and wonderfully made: marvelous are thy works; and that my soul knoweth right well. My substance [embryonic mass] was not hid from thee, when I was made in secret . . . Thine eyes did see my substance, yet being unperfect; and in thy book all my members were written, which in continuance were fashioned . . . How precious also are thy thoughts unto me, O God! how great is the sum of them!" (Psalm 139:13-17).

This passage of Scripture teaches that even our physical appearance and our bodily members are designed by God himself. You are not an "accident" or the product of chance. You are the uniquely designed creature of God. Even men like Moses (speech impediment) and Paul ("thorn in the flesh") learned that God makes the deaf, dumb, and blind (cf. Ex. 4:11) for his glory and that his sufficient grace is available to sustain us in our weaknesses (2 Cor. 12:7-10). Your physical limitations are God-given to help develop the character qualities of your life. Do not let them become a source of bitterness.

TEST YOURSELF: HOW IS A HEALTHY SELF-CONCEPT BUILT INTO A CHILD?

1. With the parent's voice.

___ Yes ___ No Do I speak my child's name with pleasure?

___ Yes ___ No Do I use my child's real name rather than a demeaning nickname?

___ Yes ___ No Do I use words like "stupid, naughty, messy, selfish, etc." on my children?

___ Yes ___ No Do I frequently yell at my child when I want him to do something?

___ Yes ___ No Do I talk about my child in positive ways when he is listening?

2. With the parent's facial expression.

___ Yes ___ No Do I communicate to my child with eye contact?

___ Yes ___ No Do I communicate with my child through my facial expression?

3. Through proper nonverbal communication.

___ Yes ___ No Do I cause my child to feel loved by me?

___ Yes ___ No Do I make my child think I think his work is juvenile or childish?

4. Through avoiding comparison.

___ Yes ___ No Do I compare my child with other children?

____ Yes ____ No Do I feel self-conscious about something unchangeable about my child?

____ Yes ____ No Do I use my child to satisfy my own unfulfilled ambitions?

5. By being lavish in praise and appreciation.

____ Yes ____ No Do I praise my child for positive inner qualities or actions I appreciate?

____ Yes ____ No Do I make only positive comments about my child when he is listening?

6. By training to assume responsibility.

____ Yes ____ No Do I fail in my example of responsibility by making promises to my child and forgetting to keep them?

____ Yes ____ No Does my child have assigned responsibilities within our home?

____ Yes ____ No Do I make sure he follows through with his responsibilities?

7. By putting courtesy first.

____ Yes ____ No Do I treat my child with courtesy?

____ Yes ____ No Do I express an interest in things my child wants to share with me?

REMEMBER, you represent Jesus Christ's leadership and authority to your child. He will formulate his confidence in God and himself from your success in instilling a healthy self-concept in him.

HOW DO I BEGIN?

1. Establish in your child's mind that a change in operation is taking place.

2. Express gratitude that he is your child and God's special gift to you.

3. Acknowledge your failure in not accepting your child as God's unique design.

4. Ask his forgiveness for your past mistakes.

5. Begin immediately to apply these guidelines.

Effective change does not need to be accomplished by a total shock tactic. Change is best accomplished by preparing the family for it. Parents who are convinced of the need for some changes should also prepare their family for those changes. The value to be gained in changing wrong patterns can be lost by wrongly changing those patterns. Your sensitivity to the will of God and the needs of your family will determine your commitment to doing whatever is necessary to produce the best results both now and in the future.

SOMETHING TO THINK ABOUT

Which comes more easily to me?

_____ *Love*   _____ *Discipline*

Which do I need to work on more?

_____ *Love*   _____ *Discipline*

Which did my parents tend toward?

*Father*_____

*Mother*_____

Am I like them or am I reacting to what they were like? __

_____

In what ways am I hurting my child's self-image? _____

_____

_____

What changes should I make to correct this? _____

_____

_____

_____

The Total Parent: The Authoritative Balance

Briefly explain your philosophy of child discipline: ____

_____

_____

_____

_____

_____

6/Discipline That Works!

Does God really keep his promises to us? Of course he does. The Bible reminds us that the Lord "is not a man that he should lie." God has made a blessed promise to your family and he plans to keep it. The promise is found in Proverbs 22:6: "Train up a child in the way he should go: and when he is old, he will not depart from it."

GOD'S FORMULA FOR A SUCCESSFUL FAMILY

Many parents want to rephrase that promise to read: "Train up a child, and when he becomes a teenager, he will go astray, but eventually he will come back when he is old." There is a great danger in trying to interpret Scripture in the light of one's own experience, rather than interpreting our experiences in the light of God's Word.

If you were able to read the Hebrew in which this promise was originally given, you would discover that it carries the meaning: "As he is growing older, he will not depart." The promise of God is sure. He will not fail. What if your child does not turn out right? The only scriptural conclusion is that you have not trained him right.

"TRAINING": LOVE AND DISCIPLINE

Training involves instructing, but it includes more than that. When one trains a dog he does not merely talk to it. He usually applies the rolled up newspaper! "Training" includes both instruction and discipline. In Ephesians 6:4, the Apostle Paul warns: "And, ye fathers, provoke not your children to wrath: but bring them up in the nurture [discipline] and admonition [instruction] of the Lord." When a parent does not balance his discipline with scriptural instruction, he will ultimately provoke his children to rebellion. A parent's discipline cannot be based upon personal opinion (the teenager will always challenge this). Instruction is the foundation of discipline and it must be based upon the Word of God.

SPANKING CHILDREN: DOES IT REALLY WORK?

There can be no doubt that the Bible strongly and clearly advises parents to spank their disobedient children. "Spare the rod and spoil the child" is a scriptural adage known by saved and unsaved people alike. The writer of Proverbs stated the issue clearly when he said, "He that spareth his rod hateth his son: but he that loveth him chasteneth him betimes" (Prov. 13:24).

DISCIPLINE IS MORE THAN TALKING

Discipline is a necessary responsibility of every parent. However, discipline can be improperly applied. There are three essential elements of the parent-child relationship:

INSTRUCTION (what you say)

INFLUENCE (what you do)

IMAGE (what you are)

Many parents mistakenly assume that child discipline is simply instructing children by telling them what to do. Often, brokenhearted parents have related to me the failure of the children with the lamentable, "But I told them what to do!" Remember, instruction is only part of the process. Your actions may have contradicted your instruction.

THE PARENT IS THE KEY

A mother may instruct her daughter about the importance of modesty, yet dress immodestly herself. Her "image" contradicts her instruction and, therefore, confuses the child. A father may tell his son not to smoke or drink, when he does both. The influence of his actions contradicts his instruction. One's "image" and "influence" may contradict his instruction and his child may follow his parent's influence rather than his instruction.

Effective discipline begins with the parent. He must discipline himself to be willing to consistently discipline his child every time he disobeys. Then, he must be willing to use the rod! Nowhere does the Bible teach a parent to spank with his hand. To the contrary, every reference in Scripture to discipline refers to using a neutral object (Psa. 89:32; Prov. 10:13; 22:15; 23:13; 26:3; Is. 10:5; 1 Cor. 4:21).

THE RIGHT AND WRONG WAY TO SPANK

In your child's mind your hand is associated with you. You reach out to your child and communicate love to him by touch. In fact, psychologists have discovered that if a baby is never touched, it will die. Touching expresses love. The time you spent holding, cuddling, or nursing your children, you were communicating love to them.

When the parent's hand turns against the child, he breaks the chain of his love. The use of a neutral object stands between the parent and the child as a token of the seriousness and responsibility of the child's disobedience. People often say to me, "But I spank my children all the time and it doesn't work!" When I ask them, "With what do you spank them?" their reply is always the same. "Well, with my hand." Use a rod and be serious and sincere in your attitude. Discipline is not punishment; it is correction. "Foolishness is bound in the heart of a child, but the rod of correction shall drive it far from him" (Prov. 22:13). However, the Bible further reminds us: "And, ye fathers, provoke not your children to wrath: but bring them up in the nurture and admonition of the Lord" (Eph. 6:4).

The Bible clearly teaches that there is a right way and a wrong way to discipline children. In fact, there is a right and wrong way to spank children. One method produces lasting and life-changing results while the other merely provokes more disobedience.

BALANCE: INSTRUCTION AND DISCIPLINE

Notice the two key elements of parental discipline mentioned in Ephesians 6:4: "nurture" and "admonition." The word "nurture" means discipline and the word "admonition" means instruction. If these are not used in proper balance, the child may easily be provoked to rebellion. In Proverbs 22:6 we read that familiar promise: "Train up a child in the way he should go: and when he is old, he will not depart from it." Many parents, looking at their own failures, have been tempted to interpret this promise as only applying to old age. You train him they say, and as he grows up, he will probably wander away, but eventually (in old age) he will return to the Lord. What kind of promise is that? What kind of example would that be of a Christian having his family in submission to Christ? The promise of Proverbs 22:6 is much greater than that. The original Hebrew clearly says: "as he is growing older, he will not depart." God's promise is sure throughout the life of the child (including his teenage and adult years). If you train your child properly, he will not depart from that training.

Training involves more than merely talking. "Training," in a biblical sense, is the combination of instruction and discipline. Every parent "trains" his child (one way or another); whether he intends to or not. You are either training him to obey you the first time you speak or the fourth time or the tenth time! Nevertheless, you are training (or "conditioning") his response.

YELLING = FAILURE

If a parent yells at his children several times before disciplining them, he is actually training them not to obey the first few times he speaks to them. Your child can learn to obey you the first time you speak just as easily as he can the ninth time. The key to discipline is not the child. It is the parent!

Sooner or later, every parent will discipline his child. Every time you threaten without acting, however, you "train" your child not to obey. The more a parent uses his mouth (yelling, threatening, etc.) the less effective he is with his discipline. Nowhere does the Bible teach us to yell at our children. Every time the Scripture refers to discipline it mentions spanking!

Most psychologists, while recognizing today's teenage generation as the most intelligent of all time, readily admit that it is also the most irresponsible. The recent Watergate tragedy is a perfect example of how deeply personal irresponsibility has affected our society. Proper discipline reinforces a sense of responsibility in the individual child. It teaches him that he is responsible for his actions. When he learns that he cannot disobey and get away with it, he will develop a more responsible attitude.

LACK OF DISCIPLINE = IRRESPONSIBILITY

A lack of discipline produces irresponsibility in children. Today's "irresponsible generation" is the result of the failure of the last generation's discipline. The anti-spanking philosophy, so popular during the last two decades, is now being opposed by most psychologists and educators. It has always been contradicted by Scripture (cf. Prov. 10:13; 13:24; 29:15; Heb.

12:6). In Proverbs 22:15 we read, "Foolishness is bound in the heart of a child; but the rod of correction shall drive it far from him."

The rod stands as a neutral object between the parent and child, whereas the hand is a direct part of the parent. With your hands you communicate love to your child through touch. When that hand turns against him, he becomes confused and tends to resist it. In fact, some parents actually end up "wrestling" with their own children while attempting to discipline them.

Discipline has correction as its goal (not just punishment). All the hollering and swatting in the world are useless if they fall short of correcting the child's disobedience. The key to success is seriousness and sincerity, not severity (the rod need not be a baseball bat in order to do the job).

FIVE STEPS TO EFFECTIVE DISCIPLINE

Many concerned parents are searching for a method of effective discipline for their children. During the past two decades, many psychologists have advised against physical discipline for fear of "sublimating the child's creativity." As a result of this unscriptural philosophy, we have reaped a generation of irresponsible and undisciplined young people.

One of the strongest advocates against spanking was Dr. Spock, who has recently retracted his earlier opinion. In the meantime, however, hundreds of thousands of youngsters have been influenced by his former views. The Christian parent (and grandparent) cannot afford to "hodge-podge" together bits of information from several conflicting sources. As never before, we need to rely on the Bible's own prescription for child discipline.

I. Instruction: Proper discipline begins with instruction. In Ephesians 6:4, we read: "And, ye fathers, provoke not your children to wrath: but bring them up in the nurture [discipline] and admonition [instruction] of the Lord." The balance of instruction and discipline are BOTH necessary in "not provoking" rebellion from the child.

All discipline must be founded upon proper instruction (Proverbs 22:6). This should include direction in regard to right-wrong and good-bad actions. Too many parents do not teach their children what they expect of them. The child needs to know this, so that when he disobeys, he will realize that he is receiving the discipline that he deserves. Another common problem is that parents often base their instruction and moral values upon their own personal opinion . . . "Well this is how I had to do it . . . don't ask why, just do it because I say so!"

Modern public education will teach your child to challenge your opinion. The foundation of a parent's instruction needs to be far more absolute and authoritative. Your instruction in righteousness to your children needs to be based upon the infallible truths of God's Word.

As a parent, you need to bring your child's disobedience to the Scriptures—causing him to see that he has broken God's laws as well as yours. He needs to understand the principles of Scripture that form the foundation of your discipline.

II. Reinforcement: With smaller children you will find that it is often effective to remind the child of your previous instruction and the penalty for disobedience. By using reinforcement to the instruction you may enhance the child's responsibility for his disobedience. He must conclude, "They told me not to do it; they reminded me not to do it, and I did it anyway. Therefore, I deserve the discipline I am receiving."

III. Correction: The ultimate goal of discipline is not punishment. It is correction! Wrong attitudes and actions must be corrected into right ones. Any discipline that falls short of correction has not gone far enough.

Discipline that goes all the way to the point of correction teaches the child that he is responsible for his wrong actions. A lack of proper discipline will always result in an irresponsible attitude in the child. This effect may carry over into the child's spiritual life as well. The youngster who "learns" that he can disobey his parents and "get away with it," will also come to think that he can sin against God and go unpunished.

IV. Restitution: It is always best to establish a means of restitution to "right" the wrong that has been done. This builds an attitude of repentance in the child. The Bible admonishes: "Let him that stole steal no more: but rather let him labour, working with his hands . . ." (Eph. 4:28). God's Word always recommends restitution of wrongs: clearing one's conscience through seeking forgiveness, returning stolen goods, etc.

The means of restitution should be reasonable and effective. Nothing will stop a potential liar or thief more than having to say, "I lied to you," or "I stole this."

V. Reassurance: Never hesitate to express your love and concern for a disobedient child. Your expression of love reassures him that you are not rejecting him. Do not give him the impression that you are sorry that you disciplined him (you should not be). But it is equally important to assure him that you have disciplined him because you care about him and his character development. One caution here: the one who does the disciplining should also be the one to do the loving. Do not give the impression you are sorry your mate gave the discipline. Reinforce each other's decisions. Again, remember that the key to effective discipline is YOU, not your child. Your willingness to lead your children and take responsibility for developing the character of their lives will determine the overall quality of your home.

SOMETHING TO THINK ABOUT

How would you rate your children's obedience?

____ *Excellent* ____ *Good* ____ *Fair* ____ *Poor* ____ *Help!*

Now, what kind of parental discipline are you giving him?

____ *Excellent* ____ *Good* ____ *Fair* ____ *Poor* ____ *Help!*

How often do you yell at your children?

___*100%* ___*75%* ___*50%* ___*25%* ___*0%*

How often do your children respond to your verbal commands?

___*100%* ___*75%* ___*50%* ___*25%* ___*0%*

Briefly describe your most unsuccessful attempt at discipline: _____

_____

_____

Now, describe your most successful attempt at discipline:

_____

_____

_____

What improvements should you make in your approach to disciplining your children?_____

_____

_____

_____

_____

_____

Discipline That Works!

7/Dynamic Devotions and Total Family Communication

"And ye fathers, provoke not your children to wrath: but bring them up in the nurture and admonition of the Lord." Ephesians 6:4

One of the greatest spiritual opportunities your family will ever have will be in the area of family devotions. Your children will be blessed beyond anything you can imagine by having the opportunity of praying with you and reading the Word of God as a family.

DYNAMIC DEVOTIONS: THE HEARTBEAT OF THE HOME

This matter of devotions, or "family altar" is probably the most crucial area of spiritual responsibility that any family faces. Over the years, pastors across our nation have shared with us that this is the one key area that is the greatest failure of their church people. Most Christians agree that they need to have regular devotions but simply do not know how to do it effectively. Let me share these simple and practical suggestions with you.

GETTING STARTED:

A. *Set a Definite Time.* If you start wrong, you will fail. Start right and your devotions will be a success. The key in beginning is to set a specific time for your family devotions. Otherwise, the time will slip by, and your "good intentions" will be wasted. You may have to get up earlier, stay up later, or reorganize your schedule. It will be worth any adjustment you must make.

B. *Involve Everyone.* What could be more important than the spiritual well-being of your family? There needs to be a time when every member of your family sits down together to share in family devotions. Select a time that is good for everyone, and give each person an opportunity to read the Bible and share in a time of prayer. You may want to rotate around the bale (or a circle), giving each one a time of expression and contribution.

C. *Be Consistent.* Once you begin, do not quit! It will be all the harder to start again. I would personally rather see you spend ten to fifteen minutes together every night, than to attempt thirty to sixty minutes and become "weary in well doing."

GROWING SPIRITUALLY:

A. *Develop a Meaningful Atmosphere.* Turn off the television, loud distractions from the radio, etc. If necessary, take the telephone off the hook. Make this a concentrated time of spiritual emphasis. If you are having your devotional time in connection with breakfast or supper, let the entire mealtime become a spiritually meaningful atmosphere that is conducive to God's speaking to your lives.

B. *Develop Better Bible Study.* The real goal of family devotions is personal spiritual growth for your entire family. Much of this will come from reading and applying God's Word to your lives. Do not hesitate to read the Bible itself with your children. Let them see its significant place as the inspired guideline for your family. You may want to "supplement" this with an appropriate Bible storybook for your younger children.

This is especially effective at bedtime. However, use the Bible in your devotions with your entire family. Let even your first- and second-graders (who are learning to read) share in the actual reading of simpler passages. It will thrill them to know that they too can read the Bible. This teaches them that the Scripture is not a "closed book" to them. It lets them know that God will speak to them also.

In approaching a passage of Scripture, it is important that the father read it ahead of time in order to be prepared to guide the family's study. Let each person in the family take a turn reading the passage. In your study, you want to determine:

What does the passage say?

What does it mean?

How does it apply to me?

Always make a practical application of Scripture to your family's needs. Let me suggest some examples.

Some time ago, we were reading the Book of Judges in our family devotions. It is a series of accounts of Israel's battles with her enemies. So we decided to make a list of our "enemies" (such as "cry-baby," not eating well, etc., for the children). Every day during devotions we analyzed our battles with our enemies and listed our progress. It worked amazingly well as each of us made significant improvement. As we read the accounts in Judges, we also noted that when Israel obeyed God, they were blessed, and when they disobeyed God, they were judged. We then applied this principle to our own daily conflicts.

You may want to read one of the Gospel accounts of Jesus' life, the story of the growth of the church in Acts, or a warm-hearted book like Philippians or Psalms. In each case, the use of a family Bible study notebook is almost indispensable. An excellent study can be made in Proverbs of basic character qualities. This may be an excellent way to teach your children how to discern basic character needs in themselves and others. Here is an example of several character types which appear in Proverbs.

CHARACTER	DESCRIPTION	REACTION
sinners	entice	consent not
fools	refuse instruction	be not
wise men	heed advice	follow example
"strange women"	lure with eyes	avoid/flee

C. *Develop a More Powerful Prayer Time.* Most people become bored in public or group praying simply because they are not praying for something specific. Specific praise and specific requests bring specific blessings! Do not make the prayer time unnecessarily long. Give everyone an opportunity to pray.

You may find it very helpful to develop a "Family Prayer Request Notebook." Have one section of PEOPLE that you want to pray for on a regular basis (your pastor, church workers, friends, relatives, etc.). Rotate your way through the list each week by having each family member pray for one or two people per night. In another section, have a list of MISSIONARIES that you can pray for specifically. Write to them on their fields and list specific needs for which your family may pray. In a third section, compile a list of DAILY REQUESTS. Be specific! Write down each day's prayer requests and then check them off as they are answered.

DATE	REQUESTS	ANSWERED
Mon. 3/11	Mother's sickness	X
Mon. 3/11	Johnny's test at school	X

Mon. 3/11	Neighbor's family needs	
Tues. 3/12	Safety for day at work	X
Tues. 3/12	Pastor's health	

In time, you will have a notebook filled with hundreds of check marks. As your children browse through it, they will be impressed that God answers prayer! This will also increase your praise to the Lord as you specifically recall how many prayers he is answering on your behalf.

GIVING STABILITY

The end result of consistent devotions will be spiritual stability within your family. Regular devotions will increase your children's respect for your leadership. It will build an attitude of repentance for sin and personal wrongs. A family cannot pray together while holding onto bitterness and grudges. The secure atmosphere of regular spiritual family communication will set your children at rest in their souls. There is much to be accomplished in the lifetime of your family. So get to the task with discipline and determination. "Oh, how I love thy law! it is my meditation all the day" (Psa. 119:97).

BRIDGE TO CONFLICTS

The foundation of family communication through prayer and regular devotions will create an atmosphere of open spiritual expression. This will help pave the way for a more direct dealing with conflicts and problems within your family. It is difficult to continue praying with someone with whom you are upset. Therefore, devotions prepare the family for a more honest attempt to solve its differences. No family will ever be completely devoid of differences of opinion, variation of viewpoints, and even contradiction of one another. Successful family living does not necessarily mean the elimination of all differences, but the proper handling of those differences.

SOLVING FAMILY CONFLICTS

If you really want help with your problems, God has a solution for you. Use it sincerely and properly, and you may solve any kind of family conflict (flights, past bitternesses, hurts, failures, etc.). Fill in the material below as if I were talking to you in a personal counseling situation.

1. List each member of your family: father, mother, children, etc.

_____

_____

_____

_____

2. Now, circle the names of each family member with whom you have personal conflicts.

3. Under each name you have circled, list each of their faults (especially those bothering you). Go ahead . . . be honest and fair. You will never solve these conflicts until you face them!

4. Now, under your name, list all your faults! Go ahead . . . do not just put down what you are willing to admit . . . what would another person say if he were making the list!

5. Next, look at everything you have written. How many of these conflicts has the other person caused, and how many have you caused? Remember, it is very rare for a problem to be 100 percent the other person's fault. It takes two to tangle! If it helps you visualize the problem, write down (next to each name) the percentage of wrong you feel the other person is contributing to these conflicts (the remaining percent is how much you are contributing). Now, if you will subtract about

10 percent from the other person and add it to yourself, you will probably have a more realistic picture.

6. At this point, I would ask you whether or not you really want to solve these problems. Some people do not want solutions, they merely want to cry about their problems. You will never solve your problems by crying about them unless your sorrow leads to repentance and to positive action. If you want help, there is an answer. But you must be willing to use it. The anwer is not easy, but it works!

7. No psychiatrist has ever discovered a valid answer for solving personal relationship problems other than God's answer. In fact, there is no other answer. Here it is! You must be willing to recognize that you are contributing to the conflicts between yourself and the other person. Whether you "started it" or not, you are still responsible for the wrong attitude and reaction that you have had. Therefore, in order to resolve these conflicts, you must take the responsibility for your part of the wrong and acknowledge to the other person that you have wronged him and ask his FORGIVENESS for the problem that exists between you. Sincerely seeking forgiveness builds a sense of responsibility in you and "melts" the bitterness in the other person's heart. Whatever you do, don't say: "Please forgive me of my 20 percent of the wrong!" Leave the bitter details out. You do not have to cry, but you must be SINCERE. The principle of forgiveness is God's principle, and all of his power stands behind it. Use it properly (seriously and sincerely), and it will always work! (cf. Luke 17:3, 4; Mark 11:22-25; Matt. 18:21-35; Eph. 4:32; Col. 3:13).

8. If you expect the other person to forgive you, then you must also be willing to FULLY FORGIVE him! That takes care of all 100 percent of the problem. You forgive him all the wrong he has done against you; and he forgives you all the wrong you have done against him.

Maturity is being willing to make the first move to solve family problems. Immature people never want to commit themselves until they see the response of another. A mature Christian will be willing to do whatever is necessary to benefit his family. Such a person is not worried about WHO is right or wrong, but WHAT is right or wrong. The mature person is concerned about others and is willing to do whatever is right to correct a problem. He or she will want to resolve differences, bring peace, and restore relationships (cf. Matt 5:9). Scripture admonishes: "Ye which are spiritual, restore . . . in the spirit of meekness" (Gal 6:1).

HOW TO BE A SPIRIT-FILLED PARENT

The Holy Spirit can empower you to be a successful parent and a successful partner! There is much talk today about the power and ministry of the Spirit. He is God the Perfector. His ministry is to convict us of sin, call us to Christ, and empower us to live for him.

The Apostle Paul urges us: "And be not drunk with wine, wherein is excess; but be [continually] filled with the Spirit" (Eph. 5:18). Why did he choose being "drunk" as a parallel to being "filled" with the Spirit? When a person is drunk, he is "filled" with alcohol and it controls his actions. Thus, when one is filled with the Holy Spirit, he is totally controlled by him. The evidence of his control is obedience to God's Word!

Be cautious of those who try to make some outward "manifestation" the evidence of Spirit-filling. Anyone can imitate outward activity (shouting, moaning, groaning, falling, etc.). No one can imitate genuine heart obedience to God! Jesus said that the Holy Spirit would reprove the world of sin, righteousness, and judgment (John 16:8). As he convicts us of sin, he then leads us to obedience unto righteousness.

The true evidence of the filling of the Holy Spirit is genuine obedience. How does this affect the Spirit-filled parent? In order to be such, the parent must obey the directions of the Word of God for the family. This means that husbands must be leaders and wives must be submissive (Eph. 5:21-25) in order to be Spirit-filled.

God's "chain of command" must be followed in order for the parent to be controlled by God. Many women claim to have the "gift of the Spirit," etc., and yet are living in open disobedience to their husbands. They cannot be Spirit-filled women and disobey the clear direction of God's Word. Husbands who do not "love their wives" and lead their families are not Spirit-filled men.

If you really desire the power of God on your family and in your life, obey the leading of the Holy Spirit through the Word of God. Apply the principles of God to yourself and your family, and you will experience his fullest blessings. The Bible is your "manual for living" and its truths must become the standards for your family's practice. The Word of God is the revealer of the thoughts and intents of the heart (Heb. 4:12). As we obey its directions, we fulfill the will of God for our lives.

"But the mercy of the Lord is from everlasting to everlasting upon them that fear him, and his righteousness unto children's children." Psalm 103:17

SOMETHING TO THINK ABOUT

Rate the consistency of your family devotions:

____*100* ____*80* ____*60* ____*50* ____*40* ____*20* ____*0*

Rate the quality of your family devotions:

____*100* ____*80* ____*60* ____*50* ____*40* ____*20* ____*0*

Now the rate of your family's total spiritual condition:

____*100* ____*80* ____*60* ____*50* ____*40* ____*20* ____*0*

How do the previous three answers compare?_____

What immediate improvements should be made in your family devotions? _____

_____

_____

_____

What internal conflicts are hindering the spiritual growth of your family? _____

_____

_____

_____

What steps should you take to help correct them? _____

_____

_____

Am I mature enough to take the responsibility for solving this problem?

____ *Yes*　　____ *No*

Am I willing to go to the other person(s) immediately and make things "right"?

____ *Yes*　　____ *No*

Is our family at peace with one another?

____ *Yes*　　____ *No*

Is Christ really in control of our family?

____ *Yes*　　____ *No*

Can I have the power of the Holy Spirit without being controlled by him?

____ *Yes*　　____ *No*

8/Developing Total Family Togetherness

A total family is one that has developed a deep sense of "togetherness." It is a family in which truth prevails as a standard for ethical living, and love permeates the attitude with which those standards are enforced. A total family is one that loves God, loves his Word, and loves its individual members.

LEARNING TO LOVE

This missing ingredient in the world today is genuine love. A popular song once said, "What the world needs now is love." Not only does the world with its harshness, cruelty, and "dog-eat-dog" philosophy need love, but so does the average Christian family. We often emphasize that genuine revival must begin at home. Even in the "sanctuary" of our own home, however, we often discover little evidence of genuine Christian love. Your family can never really have too much love. The question is, does it have enough?

IF LOVE IS NOT JUST EMOTION, THEN WHAT IS IT?

A man once came to me for counsel regarding his family problems. He began by stating that his family lacked real love and loving concern for each other. But then he quickly added, "But I just don't want it to be a bunch of emotion!" His statement raises the question, what is real love and how is it expressed? Jesus had much to say about love. So much in fact that the liberal thinking element of the church tended to think that love alone was Jesus' message of salvation. Fundamental conservative preachers have rightly understood that this was not true. However, in reacting to the liberal distortion of Christ's message, they may be neglecting the proper value of love. A proper understanding, though, of the entire message of the Bible reveals that love is in reality the dynamic of the Christian life.

LOVE YOUR WIFE, LOVE YOUR NEIGHBOR, LOVE YOUR ENEMY, LOVE EVERYBODY!

When the Apostle Paul told the Christian husband to love his wife (Eph. 5:25), that was understandably justified. But the New Testament message goes far beyond this. We are not only to love our own family members, but we as a family are to love other families, including our neighbors and even our enemies. Since love is the first fruit of the Holy Spirit (Gal. 5:22), and since every Christian who is genuinely born again is born of the Spirit, then every true believer has the potential to produce the quality and actions of love. In other words, there is no excuse for not loving any person that God may bring across the path of your life. A young couple once complained to me, "We know that we are both saved, but the problem is we just don't love each other any more!" Scripturally, that statement cannot be true. It is a contradiction of what God has promised when he said that love is the ultimate by-product of genuine conversion. In 1 John, the Bible clearly says, "We know that we have passed from death unto life because we love the brethren. He that loveth not his brother, abideth in death." There is no excuse for not loving.

HOW DO YOU LOVE AN ENEMY? HOW DO YOU LOVE ANYBODY?

Most of us readily admit that love is a genuine expression of the Christian life. Most of us acknowledge that we need to learn to be more loving and most of our family members would readily agree. If love is not just an emotion, though it may involve an expression of our emotions, then what is it? When Jesus told his disciples to love their enemies, what did he expect them to do? Hug and kiss? Feel ooey and gooey? No! He told them how to love them: "Love your enemies, bless them that curse you, do good to them that hate you." In other words, his plan is to love and give. You love your enemy by "giving him a cup of cold water in Jesus' name." You love him by pleasing him. You love him by praying for him (not against him).

It is at this point that we really get down to the basics of what loving is all about. Loving someone involves giving to them through acts of kindness. I asked that young couple, "How can you hope to stand before the Lord one day and say, 'we just don't love each other,' when God expects you to love even your worst enemy?" Loving your wife or husband or children must involve the same kind of love response that loving your enemy does, and that means learning to give to them whatever they need in order to build and develop their lives. "Husbands, love your wives, even as Christ also loved the church, and gave himself for it." You see, the answer has been there in the Bible all along. When we do not feel the emotion of love, that is never an excuse for some very unloving ways and you may feel that emotionally your love has been drained. Here is where many couples make a serious mistake. They wait for the emotion of love to return by itself. Emotions do not usually repair themselves. They are reestablished by right actions!

When you do not feel the emotion of love, do not forget that feelings are produced by actions and thoughts. An action of love will always bring with it a feeling of love. Your family needs your love. They need you to give them the time, attention, and concern that is necessary to produce the security of true love. They also need the total commitment of your heart attitude. When your thoughts are constantly on your job, finances, responsibilities, relatives, hobbies, etc., they will not center on your family's needs. When a husband or wife allows the great majority of his or her thoughts to be on things outside the home, there will generally be a lack of attention on things within the home.

Selfish living for one's own personal gratification produces bitter and selfish attitudes within a family. Selfish people are never sacrificial people. Learning to love means learning to love others. It involves the sacrifice of self-denial.

DEVELOPING SPIRITUAL GROWTH IN YOUR FAMILY

It is the last inning of a tie baseball game. There is a runner on third base with one out. A pinch hitter steps into the batter's box to face the opposing pitcher. The windup . . . the pitch . . . the hitter squares off to bunt. He drops a perfect bunt down the third baseline as the runner breaks toward home plate. The pitcher races toward the ball, but fields it too late. The run scores! The game has been won by a sacrifice bunt.

SACRIFICE IS A PART OF LIVING

From the very beginning of man's struggle with sin, God has provided a means of sacrifice. First, the animal sacrifices of the Old Testament and later the eternal sacrifice of Christ's death for our sins. Salvation is free but is not cheap. It cost God his very best. It cost Jesus his life!

Our Lord challenged his followers with these words: "If any man will come after me, let him deny himself, and take up his cross daily, and follow me" (Luke 9:23). Self-sacrifice will not save anyone, but it is a vital part of Christian living. The psalmist said, "Offer the sacrifices of righteousness and put your trust in the Lord." Sacrifice is such a vital part of our lives that it affects us daily. Someone sacrificed to put you through school ... someone sacrificed to build a Bible-preaching church where you could hear the gospel. Others' sacrifices have been used of God to mold and shape your life.

WHAT ARE YOU SACRIFICING FOR YOUR FAMILY?

"I'm just so busy, I can't seem to find time to pray with my family." Have you ever heard someone say that? Have you ever said it? What is the real problem? Sacrifice! Everyone seems to want a 1-2-3 quick and easy step to instant spiritual success without sacrifice. Yet it is the discipline of sacrifice that determines that success. David once said, "How can I give the Lord that which costs me nothing?" What is the cost you will have to pay for the blessing of God on your home?

TIME: Spending quality time with your family is vital if they are to be assured of your love. We sacrifice time to attend baseball games, birthday parties, weddings, graduations ... we spend hours eating in restaurants and watching television. How much time are you willing to spend with your family?

TITHE: "But pastor, I just can't afford to tithe," one of my church members once complained. "No," I replied, "you cannot afford not to tithe." You are not only robbing God, but your own family. The more you give, the more God will give to you. Teach your children the quality of unselfishness by the discipline of tithing.

TALENT: Each one of us has certain God-given talents and spiritual gifts that God expects us to use for the full benefit of our families. Sometimes we can become so busy doing good for others that we neglect our own families.

TOTAL OBEDIENCE: No lesson in obedience is greater than the example of our own lives. If you want your children to obey God and obey you, they must see you obeying God's authority over your life. Are you willing to sacrifice your own willful choices for total obedience to God?

Sacrifice is the greatest opportunity of the Christian life ... it demands the strength of Christian character, the courage of conviction and determination of a will submitted to the will of God. When C. T. Studd, the famous British missionary, was converted, he acknowledged: "If Jesus Christ has done all of this for me, there is no sacrifice too great that I can make for him."

PERSONAL DISCIPLINE
AND SPIRITUAL GROWTH

Spiritual growth does not just happen, it comes as a result of personal discipline in the believer's life. The individual Christian is to "cleanse his heart, be filled with the Spirit, let the peace of God rule in your hearts, building yourself up in the faith."

In other words, while his spiritual growth is a result of the work of the Spirit of God in his life, the individual Christian nevertheless has a personal responsibility to develop that growth. Your family will never become a totally spiritual family by simply attending church. Your spiritual experience must become a vital part of your daily experience as a family. It must go beyond what happens on Sunday morning. Your children are looking to your life as an example of commitment to something for which life is worth living. They are not interested in following vague ideals, they are interested in giving their lives to something for which life is worth giving itself. The extent of your commitment to the lordship of Christ will determine in effect the extent of your family's commitment.

Dad, you more than anyone else in the family, are the key to God's blessing in the home. Your wife and children deserve a spiritual leader who loves them and who loves God with all his heart. They need a father who is willing to give of himself to lead their lives and to meet their needs. Mom, your family needs and deserves a mother with a willing and cooperative spirit, who uses her creative energy to complement (not conflict with) her husband's leadership. Young people, your parents need your willing obedience and cooperation to make the atmosphere of your home what God intends for it to be—a total family!

In the days of ancient Israel, as God was bringing a nation to birth, Joshua proclaimed: "But as for me and my house, we will serve the Lord" (Josh. 24:15). Just as the ancient leaders of God's people determined to lead their families into the full blessing of the Lord, so you must determine in your heart to do the same. If you really want to have a family that is growing spiritually you must be willing to lead that family in Bible study, prayer, devotions, discipline, and spiritual decision-making. Spiritual families are made, not born. Spiritual growth does not just happen, it is developed by determined effort of Spirit-filled leadership. The same principle is true in the family. Your leadership will bring the power and blessing of God on your family, or your lack of leadership will leave your family in confusion and frustration. Determine right now to let God lead you into the full blessing that he has for your family.

FAMILY LOVE AND TOTAL TOGETHERNESS

The deep and abiding unity which is necessary to permanent family stability rests upon genuine love. Every newlywed promises to "love, till death do us part." However, our faulty emotional definition of love causes people to mean: "If I keep feeling love, I will keep loving you." Thus, when the feeling is "gone" the commitment ceases. That is why God's concept of love is not a feeling to be felt, but a quality to be developed. Real love is a fruit of the Holy Spirit (Gal.

5:22). Love is God's essential ingredient for a happy home. Without love, no amount of material prosperity or social prestige can make a marriage a blessed experience. Since God is the source of all love, it is vital that one have a personal relationship with him through the saving work of Christ. The Apostle Paul said: "Husbands, love your wives even as Christ also loved the church and gave himself for it" (Eph. 5:25).

THE SOURCE OF LOVE

In writing to Timothy, the Apostle Paul said: "Now the end of the commandment is charity [love] out of a pure heart, and of a good conscience, and of faith unfeigned" (1 Tim. 1:5). This kind of love may be expressed only by a born-again believer since it comes from God himself.

Pure Heart
Clear Conscience } **LOVE**
Genuine Faith

In 1 Corinthians 13, we see the Bible's fullest definition of love: It is kind, considerate, unselfish, invincible; it is not envious, arrogant, rude, selfish, irritable, or suspicious. God's kind of love is the opposite of the self-gratifying love of the world. This definition makes it clear that the unsaved person cannot really express true love, since his heart has never been cleansed by Christ. In the original Greek language three different words were used to express the idea of "love."

> *eros*—human love (emotional)
> *phileo*—brotherly love (friendship)
> *agape*—divine love (spiritual)

Any person may experience human love or "brotherly" love, but only the Christian has divine love. *Agape* love is the first fruit of the Holy Spirit (Gal. 5:22). It is given by God to his children. The word "love" (or charity) in 1 Timothy 1:5 is the Greek work *agape*. This kind of love differs from human love in that it is unlimited love. It is not restricted to the response of the other person. God loved us while we were yet in our sins. He first loved us before we ever responded to his love. Jesus told us to love our enemies and those that despitefully use us. Only a person filled with *agape* love can do that.

Even in a dating relationship, one's expression of "love" will determine the nature of the relationship.

GOD'S WAY		MAN'S WAY	
Spirit:	unity of heart because both are saved.	Dating:	physical involvement as basis of friendship.
Soul:	unity of mind.	Engagement:	more physical involvement, self-defense to compensate for guilt.
Body:	unity of physical selves: become "one flesh."	Marriage:	transfer guilt and frustrations of past; distrust one another. Emphasis on physical and material things.

GOD'S DIRECTION TO DATING COUPLES

The Bible clearly spells out God's direction to the single, dating couple regarding sexual involvement. In 1 Thessalonians 4:3-6, we read:

> *For this is the will of God, even your sanctification, that ye should abstain from fornication: that every one of you should know how to possess his vessel [body] in sanctification and honor; not in the lust of concupiscence [evil desires], even as the Gentiles which know not God: that no man go beyond and defraud his brother in any matter . . .*

The passage clearly condemns fornication (sexual involvement outside of marriage and especially before marriage). Here we are told clearly that it is the "will of God" to abstain from fornication. Premarital sex causes the couple to defraud each other and hurt their marriage relationship. The command to "possess" (or control) one's body brings the discipline necessary to avoid defrauding those you date.

To defraud someone means to "take advantage" of him or her. For example, if someone fails to make a payment on an overdue bill, he has "defrauded" on the payment. In our context, defraud means to take advantage of someone sexually. Thus, heavy physical involvement usually causes the girl to become guilty and fearful. She is generally drawn into a physical relationship because of an emotional need to be loved. This involvement defrauds the dating relationship and becomes a barrier to effective communication within marriage. Instead of enhancing communication, sex before marriage destroys communication. The "guilty" (defrauded) conscience of the couple causes them to become dishonest with each other.

The physical aggressiveness of the man often turns to passive insensitivity after marriage. All the "romancing" that was necessary to get his girl in bed is no longer necessary. Since his motives were wrong in the first place, the husband now often begins taking his wife for granted. His self-centered attitude about sex causes her to begin to doubt the genuineness of his love. "Maybe he just loves sex, and not me," she thinks. Soon she may begin to reject her husband's sexual advances. In time, as he becomes aware of her rejection, he will begin to make sexual demands on her, only confirming her doubts. As a battle of wills and self-respect ensues, she will eventually reject him totally. It is right here that many marriages are destroyed. The couples' frustrations are often so great that they refuse to discuss them. All communication begins to break down.

Eventually most husbands decide that the battle of

demanding pride is a lost cause and give it up for a more pragmatic approach. Gifts usually work best. The husband decides to buy his wife something, give in on an argument, or let her spend some extra money. Wanting these favors, the wife usually accepts the gifts and becomes a little more responsive in bed. In a sense, she is now actually "prostituting" her own husband, by exchanging sex for a gift.

GOD'S DIRECTION TO MARRIED COUPLES

Whatever the scars of past failures, God does provide help for every problem. The husband, who initiated the original problem, needs to genuinely seek his wife's forgiveness and eliminate the "game" of lukewarmness. The couple then needs to establish the three major biblical principles for married couples.

God's direction to the married couple is found in 1 Corinthians 7:2-5.

Nevertheless, to avoid fornication, let every man have his own wife and let every woman have her own husband.	God has given his full blessing upon marriage.

Principle #1: Give 100 Percent Love

Let the husband render unto the wife due benevolence: and likewise also the wife unto the husband.	Both husband and wife must contribute a full and honest expression of love and kindness to one another.

Principle #2: Your Body Belongs to Your Mate

The wife hath not the power of her own body, but the husband: and likewise also the husband hath not power of his own body but the wife.	Neither partner has the "right" to sexually reject his mate.

Principle #3: Do Not Defraud By Abstaining

Defraud ye not one the other, except it be with consent for a time, that ye may give yourselves to fasting and prayer; and come together again, that Satan tempt you not for your incontinency.

Sexual expression of love should be regular and consistent. Abstinence leads to temptation.

In this section of Scripture we discover that God's blessing is upon total marriage. It is not his will for couples to have to suffer with "half" a marriage. Sexual abstinence and a lack of total sexual expression and communication violate the very purpose of the physical aspect of marriage. Such an attitude leads to defrauding within marriage. To live with someone and to sleep in the same bed avoiding sexual contact is just as wrong as it is for an unmarried couple to have sex together. Such an approach to marriage denies the clear teaching of the Word of God; 1 Corinthians 7:2-5, is just as clear as John 3:16. It is the fundamental manifesto of Christian marital sex ethics. In a world overrun with sexual corruption, this is God's provision against temptation. By having the right relationship sexually, the couple eliminates the potential of temptation from an ungodly world.

The Bible is not an old, antiquated book that does not speak to the real issues of life. It is as up-to-date as tomorrow morning's newspaper will be when it comes out! Learn to trust its directions. Believe it and live it, and your marriage relationship can be revolutionized for good. Having a properly consistent personal relationship will slam shut the "door of temptation" and bring the blessing of true sexual harmony in your home.

SOMETHING TO THINK ABOUT
What is your personal definition of "love"? _____

_____

_____

_____

What is the biblical definition of love? (See 1 Corinthians 13; 1 Tim 1:5; Eph. 5:25; John 3:16.) _____

_____

_____

How far afield is your definition from God's definition?___
_____

List five major ways in which you outwardly show genuine love to your family:

1. _____

2. _____

3. _____

4. _____

5. _____

List the five greatest sacrifices you have ever made for your family.

1. _____

2. _____

3. _____

4. _____

5. _____

How well am I really "ministering" to the personal and sexual needs of any mate?

____ *very well* ____ *fair* ____ *insufficient* ____ *poor*

How does my mate respond sexually to me?

____ *very well* ____ *fair* ____ *insufficient* ____ *poor*

Is this causing problems in other areas of my marriage? ___

_____

Developing Total Family Togetherness

What areas? _____

In what ways may I improve my contribution to our personal relationship?

_____

_____

_____

9/Special Projects: The Teenager and the Total Family

Teenagers are those exciting and sometimes unusual young people between the ages of twelve and twenty. In the most crucial years of their lives they possess the potential to change the world in which we live or to virtually destroy it. During the eight years of a teenager's life he will make nearly every important decision affecting his entire future. Conflicts between parents and teenagers are not uncommon during these difficult years, as the teenager grows from childhood dependence toward young adult independence. A teenager is ascending in independence and a parent is becoming increasingly dependent upon his family. When these two lines intersect one another (usually about the time the teenager is fourteen) problems often result.

All too often, an irate parent will bring a teenager into my office, throw him down in a chair, and in essence imply that: "For eighteen years I have not been able to control this monster. Now please do something with him in the next thirty minutes!" Problems that take years to develop are not corrected in a matter of moments. However, this does not mean that there is not immediate help available to solve conflicts between parents and teenagers.

CLOSING THE GENERATION GAP

In the Bible, God referred to all believers as being a "chosen generation" (1 Pet. 2:9). It is clear in this passage that God deals with all born-again Christians as part of the same generation. Therefore, there is no "generation gap" as far as God is concerned. The Christian teenager and the Christian parent have every potential to resolve conflicts that exist between them because the Spirit of God lives in both of them. The saved teenager who has unsaved parents must become the spiritual example to those parents. As a teenager, you will never win your parents to Christ if you continue to disobey them and use your Christianity as an excuse for rebellion or rejection of their authority. Scripture clearly says, "Children, obey your parents in the Lord, for this is right" (Eph. 6:1).

The passage does not designate whether or not the parent is a Christian or whether or not the teenager agrees with his parents' decisions. It simply says that the teenager is to be obedient toward his parents. While obedience is the ideal standard of the Word of God, it often is not the real experience of many Christian families.

The major cause of conflict between young people and their parents is usually spiritual failure on the part of the parent. Whether we like it or not, our children tend to reproduce our basic life style. You cannot expect your children to rise above the spiritual standards of your own life. If you do not want your kids to smoke, don't smoke; if you don't want your kids to drink, don't drink; if you don't want your kids to holler and curse, don't holler and curse. Your teenager will usually only rise to the spiritual level of your life. While he does not have to be the victim of your life style, he usually will be. Therefore, every parent needs to realize that his child is ultimately a product of his own attitudes and actions. If you want your children to be spiritual giants, you must lead the way!

THE CHAIN REACTION OF REBELLION

Most conflicts between teenagers and their parents begin when the parent fails to live up to the standard he has established for the family. Broken promises and negative comparisons may often hurt a child deeply. For example, comparing your child's failure to another child's success, or praising one child to the neglect of another will always result in a bitter and hurtful reaction on the part of the teenager.

Years of youth-oriented ministry have convinced me beyond a shadow of a doubt that the majority of teenagers' problems result from their being hurt by things their parents have said or done to them. It is not the teenager's fault he is hurt, but it is his fault if he harbors that hurt and allows it to turn into bitterness, which destroys his own spiritual life.

Some teenagers can tell you exactly the time, the day, the place, and the incident that happened between them and their parents that deeply hurt them and caused them to begin to reject their own families. Others cannot isolate a specific incident, but remember a long series of incidents. Either way, the problem produces the same symptoms and results. Hurt harbored in the individual's heart soon becomes bitterness and bitterness leads to communication breakdown. This is the first indication that something has gone wrong between the parent and the child. However, many parents overlook this symptom as if it were merely a "stage" through which the teenager is passing.

Many times communication breakdown results because the teenager no longer feels confident about "opening up" to his parents. He fears being hurt again, therefore he keeps his feelings and frustrations to himself. In time, bitterness turns to a loss of love and respect, which shows up in the symptom of ungratefulness. This is the second danger signal that something is going wrong in the parent-teen relationship. Teenagers are greedy enough to accept the gifts that their parents give them, but not always with the best attitude. The ungrateful spirit is produced by the inner feeling that the parent is trying to buy back the teenager's love. Thus, the teenager accepts the gift, but does so with such a bad attitude that the parent wishes he hadn't given it in the first place! This only deepens the conflict between parent and teenager, and often leads to the parent playing the "when I was a kid" theme.

Mom and Dad often go into a lengthy dissertation on all the things they had to do without when they were teenagers and how they never had bicycles and cars and baseball gloves and new dresses and stereos and television set, etc. However, parents should remember that they bought all the material items that they are now criticizing their children for having. Your child cannot effectively relate to your childhood because he did not live during that period of time. If you were born during the 1930s or 1940s and your child was not born until the 1960s, there is no way he can appreciate a generation in which he did not live, any more than you can appreciate or comprehend the 1920s!

REJECTION OF AUTHORITY

When a teenager loses love and respect for his parents he will almost automatically begin to reject their authority. This will show up in the symptom of stubbornness. The teenager will become increasingly resistant to his parents' demands and regulations upon his life. He may not yet be brave enough to openly rebel, but that is soon to follow. At this point, the parent has already been given three major flashing "danger signals" that disaster is on the way: communication breakdown, ungratefulness, and stubbornness. Each of these reactions is an indication of a deeper problem within the teenager's life. While the parent fears that rejection may be coming, it has in reality already occurred in the teenager's mind! His rejection of his parents' authority soon leads to a rejection of all other adult authority as well. The teenager now finds himself at odds with his pastor, youth director, teachers, etc.

Having rejected the authority of his parents, someone must establish a new authority factor in his life. At this point, most teenagers establish themselves as that authority. They decide that "me, myself, and I are going to run my own life. No one is going to tell me what to do . . . I'm going to do my own thing." The establishment of self-authority now sets the teenager's "establishment" at odds against his parents' established authority. This almost immediately results in open rebellion. The teenager is now out of control and will not do what his parents demand of him.

It is at this point that most parents go into panic and run to their pastor, school administrator, or the police for help! Not realizing that the problem of rebellion has been brewing under the surfaces for some time (perhaps even years), the parent usually implies that something has drastically and recently gone wrong with the teenager and expects the adult authority to agree. It is at this point that parents have their greatest difficulty taking any personal responsibility for the condition in which they find their children. You will never be able to solve a problem between parents and teenagers until the parent is willing to acknowledge that he is part of the problem and, therefore, can be part of the solution as well.

Rebellion is as serious in God's sight as witchcraft (see 1 Sam. 15:23). Nowhere does the Bible condone teenage rebellion; in fact, the Scripture speaks strongly against it. Disobedience to parents is viewed as one of the indications of a reprobate mind (Rom. 1:30) and as a sign of the ungodly generation of the "last days" (2 Tim. 3:2). While the teenager must accept personal responsibility for his sinful rebellion, the parent must also face his responsibility for "provoking his children to wrath" by his neglect or overdominance. Without the proper balance of scriptural instruction and effective discipline the teenager will overreact against his parents. Too many times the parent attempts to handle the teenager's stubbornness with arguing, and his rebellion with increased rules and demands. Neither of these are necessarily corrective discipline and often only further alienate the teenager from his parents.

FOLLOWING THE CROWD

Since the teenager is now operating on self-authority he tends to feel lonely making his own decisions and will automatically look for a psychological "support group" to justify and reinforce his rebellion. This usually shows up in the form of "wrong friends." The wrong crowd always influences him to do the wrong thing, though he may also influence them in the same direction. That is because we choose as our closest friends the people that are most like us. Whether you like it or not, your friends tell a story on you, for they reveal what you are really like.

Most people choose as their friends the people with whom they have the most in common. Because of the regulations of the family or a Christian school, your teenager may still conform outwardly to certain demands, but the attitude and appearance of his friends reveal the inner attitude of his heart. The worldly crowd will cause the teenager to sin because he needs to feel accepted by the group. The more he sins, the more he will need to justify his sin. When kids begin defending smoking, drinking, and drugs, it is obvious that they are already involved in these things or wish to be involved. Their questions are not really those of genuine intellectual interest, but those of personal defense. People tend to defend their sin and in so doing reveal what their sin problems really are!

The problem with sin is that it only has pleasure "for a season" and soon leads to guilt and depression. The more a person sins, the more guilt he will experience, and in time he will begin to condemn others in order to cover his own guilt. When teenagers begin attacking all adults as "hypocritical" they are really trying to call attention away from their own sin problems. This practice is not limited to teenagers, however. Adults often practice the same tactic. Too many times the parents begin justifying themselves and throwing verbal abuse back at their teenager's problems.

SUICIDE: NUMBER ONE TEENAGER KILLER

Sin is always self-destructive. It soon leads to depression and may lead even to thoughts of suicide. When a teenager has experimented extensively with sin he will often develop the attitude, "I have tried everything there is to try, I have done everything there is to do, and I'm not happy! I might as well be dead!" Suicide is the number one killer of America's teenagers. Thousands of young people take their lives every year because they come to the end of their emotional "rope" and decide that life is not worth living. When he believes his family and friends do not have the answer to real meaning and purpose in life, he will give up on life itself. This tragedy need not ever take place in your home in your family. You must recognize that your teenager's problems are very real and must be dealt with as such. You must also recognize that these problems began, in most cases, at home, and that YOU are as much a part of the problem as you are of the solution.

WHAT CAN A PARENT DO?

What can you do if your child is already rebelling against you? As a parent, it will be necessary to take several steps of corrective action immediately:

1. Admit your failures and seek your teenager's forgiveness for whatever you have done to hurt him so deeply as to cause his rebellious attitude. Some kids will be able to tell you exactly what you did, while others will not be sure. That hurt must be cleared up before a solution can be reached.

2. Correct the original cause of hurt as much as possible and reassure your teenager by your consistent life that you have really changed for the better. Some young people will forgive you immediately, others will tend to wait and see if you are really sincere. They have been so deeply hurt that they are afraid to trust anyone. You must convince your child by your life that you can be trusted and you do have his best interest at heart.

3. Establish a plan of action by which the family will now function. Eliminate all double standards and inconsistencies. Be willing to let your teenager tell you what he really thinks about life. You might as well know the truth and begin facing it now. Talk to him and pray with him regularly. If he or she does not want to pray with you, let them hear you pray for them. They need to be aware of genuine concern.

4. Be dependable and consistent. Once you begin a new course of action, don't quit. If you give up, so will your teenager. Stick to your plan. Acknowledge any new mistakes and keep your conscience clear with your teenager at all times, thereby taking away any "excuses" for further rebellion.

5. Live your convictions at all times. As a parent, you are the key to changing your teenager. He must see God at work in your life until he is convinced that you are for real. What God does in and through you will make all the difference in your teenager's life.

10/Special Projects: The Single Parent and the Total Family

Can a single parent have a total family? The question of how the "total family" concept relates to divorced and widowed adults is vitally important. Very few Christian books discuss the plight of the single parent. With one million new divorces each year since 1975 and a national divorce rate of 40 percent, this issue is going to have to be faced more and more by the church.

In the sense that we have defined a total family, as one with a father who leads, a mother who cooperates, and children who obey their parents, a single parent family *cannot* be a total family (any more than a husband and wife with no children may be such a family). However, a couple may experience a truly total marriage (without children). While a single parent cannot be both a father and mother, he or she can fulfill the responsibility which God has given. A widowed or divorced mother can be a total mother to her children. She may be a fulfilled and creative woman who sets a godly example of spiritual influence for her family.

Many times heartbroken husbands or wives have come to me explaining their traumatic experiences over the loss of a marriage partner who refused to reconcile with them and divorced them against their wishes. These people already feel a great sense of misery and failure. We certainly cannot minister to them if we treat them as spiritual cast-offs and further reinforce their sense of failure. Prejudice in this matter has caused some Christian workers to fail to give any help at all to people who are in great need of help. Remember, it was Jesus himself who said: "They that be whole need not a physician, but they that are sick" (Matt. 9:12).

First of all, let me emphasize that you do not have to become the victim of someone else's sin. "But, you don't understand," you say, "he left me." Your husband (or wife) may have sinned against you and hurt you deeply, but you still do not have to let your life be ruined by another person's sin.

God is the author of marriage, not divorce. He is against divorce (Matt. 5:31, 32) but he is not against the divorced person. The Scripture clearly states that the *divorcer* (not the one divorced) is responsible for breaking up the marriage. Perhaps in your case you wrongly divorced your partner before your conversion. While divorce is permanent and has limitations, it is still forgivable. There is only one "unpardonable sin"— blasphemy against the Holy Spirit. Stop blaming yourself for something you cannot change. Sin is always irrecoverable as far as its action is concerned, but not as far as its effects are concerned. If you became drunk and fell through a plate glass window and cut off your arm, you may be forgiven but you will not get your arm back. If you slander someone, you may be forgiven but that does not remove the fact of your previous sin. What it does do is remove its continuing effects.

A LIST OF DON'TS
1. Don't blame God for your circumstances (divorced or widowed).
2. Don't criticize your divorced partner in front of your

children (remember, he or she is still their parent also).

3. Don't condemn yourself for circumstances beyond your control. "I wish I had done better"; "If I had said this, maybe he would not have left"; "If I had only been there, maybe he would not have died."

4. Don't wish you were someone else (that is irresponsibly avoiding reality). Such "day-dreaming" will ruin your kids.

5. Don't speculate endlessly about what might have been if . . . . The time has come to fully accept things as they are now. If your partner left and remarried the Scripture advises not to take him back (cf. Deut. 24:1-4).

6. Don't overly "spiritualize" your problems. Your kids will see right through all that drippy talk about how you are really satisfied things worked out the way they did. Don't misquote Romans 8:28.

7. Don't excuse yourself either. It takes two to tangle. Don't put all the blame on your former partner.

8. Don't become overly dependent on the wrong people. Stay away from married men/women. Don't constantly run to your friends with your problems. It will confuse you. Learn to place your greatest dependence on the Lord himself.

9. Don't dominate your kids (so they won't turn out like you). You may drive them off by being too much of a "martyr."

10. Don't worry about the future; trust God.

ACCENTUATE YOUR POSSIBILITIES

Rather than being defeated by your situation, concentrate on what you can do effectively. If you are a woman, be a mom, don't try to be a dad to your kids. Teach them, pray with them, show a submissive spirit to male "images" in your life (your dad, brother, pastor, etc.). You can lead your children without dominating them to the point of upsetting both yourself and them. The biblical standards of successful motherhood can still be met in your single parent situation.

Salvation is the gift of God's grace to provide the forgiveness of sin and redemption that we could never provide for ourselves. God did not save you in order to make you miserable. He desires to bring life as you live in obedience to his Word. While a single parent family may not be "total," because of the missing parent, it may have the atmosphere and blessing of a total family because that parent is committed to fulfilling his/her responsibilities to the children. Make your total family experience one of joy and blessing to yourself and your children. You cannot change the past but you can change the present, and that will change the future. There are still great possibilities for your family. Believe God and live by his principles. They will change your life!

For Further Reading

Adams, J.E.
Christian Living in the Home.
Grand Rapids: Baker, 1972.

Beardsley, L. and T. Spry
The Fulfilled Woman.
Irvine: Harvest House, 1975.

Benson, D.
The Total Man.
Wheaton: Tyndale House, 1977.

Brandt, H. and H. Dowdy,
Building a Christian Home.
Wheaton: Scripture Press, 1960.

Butt, H.
The Velvet-Covered Brick.
New York: Harper & Row, 1973.

Christensen, L.
The Christian Family.
Minneapolis: Bethany Fellowship, 1970.

Dobson, J.
Dare to Discipline.
Wheaton: Tyndale House, 1970.

Evans, L.H.
Your Marriage—Duel or Duet?
Westwood, New Jersey: Revell, 1962.

Getz. G.
The Christian Home in a Changing World.
Chicago: Moody Press, 1972.

Hendricks, H.
Heaven Help the Home.
Wheaton: Victor Books, 1974.

LaHaye, T.
How to be Happy Though Married.
Wheaton: Tyndale House, 1968.

Mac Donald, G.
The Effective Father.
Wheaton: Tyndale House, 1977.
Magnificent Marriage.
Wheaton: Tyndale House, 1976.

Mack, W.
**How to Develop Deep Unity
in the Marriage Relationship.**
Philadelphia: Presbyterian & Reformed, 1977.

McDonald, C.
Creating a Successful Christian Marriage.
Grand Rapids: Baker, 1975.

Meier, P.D.
Christian Child-Rearing and Personality Development.
Grand Rapids: Baker, 1977.

Morgan, M.
The Total Woman.
Old Tappan, New Jersey: Revell, 1973.

Roberts, R.R.
God Has a Better Idea: the Home.
Winona Lake, Indiana: BMH Books, 1975.

Small, D.H.
Design for Christian Marriage.
Westwood, New Jersey: Revell, 1959.
After You've Said I Do.
Old Tappan, New Jersey: Revell, 1968.

Sproul, R.C.
Discovering the Intimate Marriage.
Minneapolis: Bethany Fellowship, 1975.

Wright, H.N.
Communication: Key to Your Marriage.
Glendale: Regal Books, 1974.